1 Finsbury Avenue

1

FA

Kenneth Powell

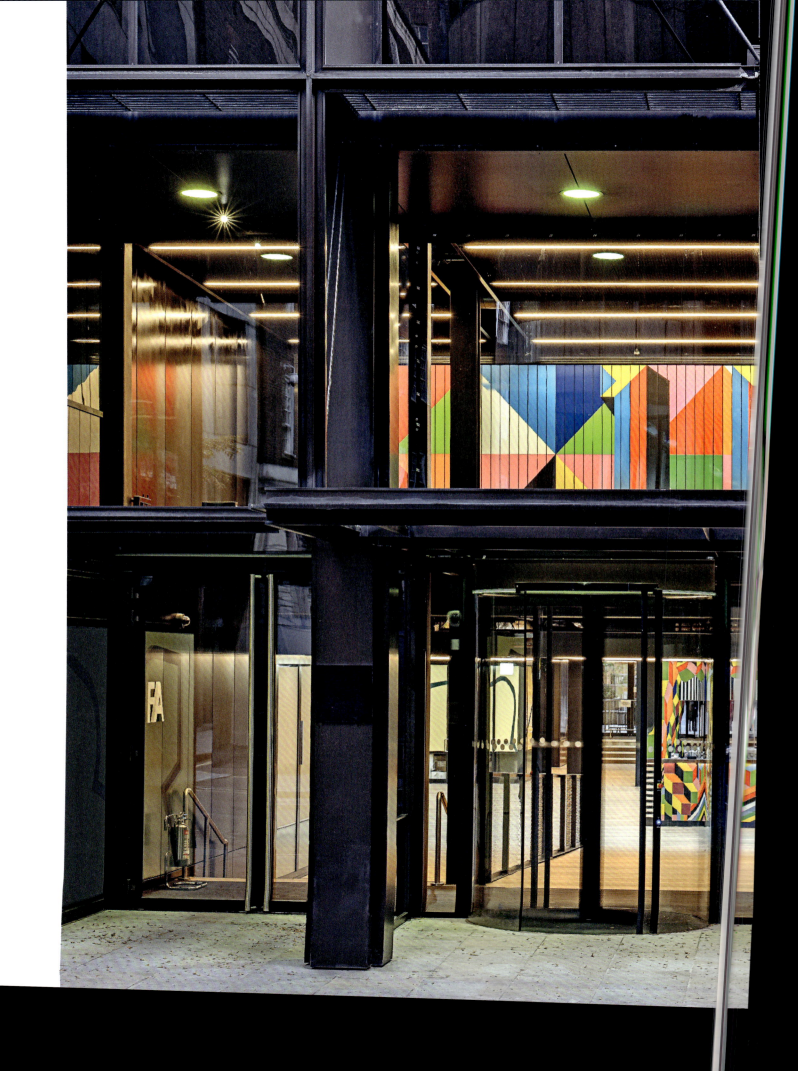

CONTENTS

Foreword by Chris Grigg 8

Foreword by Emily Gee 10

Prelude: Before the Railways 12

Afterword 122

Notes 124

Index 126

Acknowledgements & Image Credits 127

THE COMING OF
THE RAILWAYS 16

PLANNING BATTLES 26

CLIENT AND ARCHITECT 38

DESIGNING
1 FINSBURY AVENUE 50

BUILDING
1 FINSBURY AVENUE 64

THE BUILDING IN USE 82

EQUIPPING THE BUILDING
FOR THE FUTURE 98

Foreword by
CHRIS GRIGG

Chief Executive, British Land
August 2019

1 Finsbury Avenue (1FA), at the heart of Broadgate, already had a fascinating history. Originally designed by Peter Foggo of Arup Associates, the building was the catalyst for a new era of workspace across the UK when it opened in 1984.

More than 30 years later, we are delighted to have worked closely with Historic England in listing and reinvigorating this modern classic, preserving what's special about the building while adapting it to the way people live and work today so that it continues to set new trends. Working in partnership with Stirling Prize-winning architects AHMM, the iconic exterior of the building has been retained, though the ground floor has been turned into an active, accessible space where people from across Broadgate and the wider neighbourhood can meet, shop and relax in an inspirational environment, open to all.

The evolution of 1FA reflects Broadgate's wider, ongoing transformation from a financial stronghold at the centre of regulatory-driven change to a world-class, mixed-use neighbourhood, combining the creativity of Shoreditch and Spitalfields with the economic power of The City. The lively public space within 1FA is designed to accelerate such collaborations and its dual entrances honour Peter Foggo's plan for a street to run through the building, creating a vibrant, seven-day-a-week destination.

On the upper levels, the introduction of landscaped external terraces has provided outdoor spaces where people can meet and spend time, enhancing their wellbeing and bringing variety to the working day. A fresh treatment of the existing ceilings and façades has created a dramatic, raw aesthetic, providing a contemporary take on the original design.

All of this has been delivered with a commitment to sustainability – reusing, repairing and upgrading the original fabric, wherever possible – whilst significantly improving the energy performance of this historic building. The result is a reinvigorated aesthetic that has attracted international tech occupiers, who recognise the potential for the right workplace to be the physical embodiment of their brand.

As 1FA begins a new chapter, the sensitive renewal of this Grade II listed building ensures that it will continue to play an anchor role in Broadgate's transformation as a place of connection, collaboration, inspiration and excitement. We are proud to have achieved this by drawing on, and celebrating, the building's rich history.

Foreword by
EMILY GEE

Regional Director, London and South East, Historic England
August 2019

Historic England has a strong tradition of understanding and valuing the best of the recent past. Our post-war listing programme, now over 30 years old, is based on rigorous research alongside a clear and practical assigning of special interest. The first post-war building to be listed, in 1987, was – like 1 Finsbury Avenue – a commercial office in the City of London: Sir Albert Richardson's Bracken House for the *Financial Times*. Its classical style and pink sandstone, referencing the newspaper's distinctive pages, reassured a public not yet convinced about the heritage of modernity, and it paved the way for the recognition of more cutting-edge designs, like 1 Finsbury Avenue, a generation later.

The threshold for protection with recent architecture is very high indeed, but when a building meets the test of special interest in a national context, our duty is to recommend to the Government that it is recognised and celebrated on the National Heritage List. This can lead to our involvement in the management of change, and we are happy to engage with good stewardship that cares for and creatively considers a historic building's character and context. We are delighted by British Land's concept of a 'Modern Classic', and that the design interest of a special 1980s' office building would be an enticement for a range of interesting commercial tenants.

Following a complex assessment of the neighbouring Broadgate Square, where resilient working together was paramount, we worked with British Land on the listing and refurbishment of 1 Finsbury Avenue. This assessment was part of our national listing project on commercial offices, providing a clear context for understanding the building. Of the 14 offices listed in 2014, four were designed by Arup Associates – demonstrating the significance of the design practice. An important characteristic of high-tech architecture is flexibility, and this suits the way that we now do listing – empowered legally to define the extent of listing and indicate where interiors or extensions are not of special interest. This, alongside the engagement of architects who know the building well, leads to a shared understanding and creative, successful responses that work for owners, tenants and the public.

At Historic England, we are also committed to good placemaking and the role that heritage of all periods can play at the heart of thriving, interesting urban places. At 1 Finsbury Avenue, it's exciting to see the architecture and landscape of the recent past forming the framework for places that create an engaging public realm. And this in turn can contribute public value for those who visit, work and relax in this remarkable modern place.

Prelude:
BEFORE THE RAILWAYS

Prelude:
BEFORE THE RAILWAYS

'Speculative office buildings in Britain are usually horrors, planned for the meanest sort of "efficiency" and brazen in their vulgar disregard for context', wrote the critic Peter Buchanan in 1985. But, he added, 'One Finsbury Avenue is different'.[1] Even as 1 Finsbury Avenue was being completed in 1984, plans for a far larger development on land immediately to the east were well developed. Broadgate, as it became, revolutionised office development in the City of London, equipping it in due course to compete with the imminent attractions of the regenerated London Docklands, and its influence extended far beyond the Square Mile. Today, as it undergoes a process of radical renewal, Broadgate remains one of the fundamental components of the City's economy. And 1 Finsbury Avenue has been reborn as a landmark building in a rapidly changing City.

FIG.1
The London Workhouse.

The site for 1 Finsbury Avenue – and, indeed, for most of Broadgate – lay, in fact, outside the City. The local planning authority was the London Borough of Hackney – the land was brought within the City boundary only in 1994. Historically it formed part of the parish of St Leonard, Shoreditch, which abutted that of St Botolph Bishopsgate – or, more properly, Bishopsgate Without – to the west. 'Without' because St Botolph's church, ancient in origin though rebuilt in the 1720s, was located *outside* the City walls. The gate itself stood until 1761 but had long ceased to be a meaningful barrier. From the thirteenth century onwards, development – mostly small cottages, workshops, stables and taverns, plus a few more prestigious houses – sprawled northwards along what had been a Roman road with an outer bar marking the furthest extent of the City's jurisdiction. (Beyond lay the 'liberty' of Norton Folgate, a self-governing enclave which survived, remarkably, until 1899.) A densely populated suburb by the sixteenth century, this was truly 'City fringe' territory and was perceived as such even in the early 1980s when 1 Finsbury Avenue was being planned.

Amongst the institutions that the City excluded as far as possible from its confines – including theatres and brothels – were hospitals. The Hospital of St Mary of Bethlehem was founded in 1247, on land now occupied by Liverpool Street Station and the Andaz Liverpool Street Hotel. Within a century, its principal function had become the care for 'distracted persons' – that is, the insane. Run for 300 years by a religious order, 'Bedlam', as it was nicknamed, moved to Moorfields in the 1670s. Another institution that did little for the amenity of the area was the London Workhouse (fig.1), established in 1698 on the west side of Bishopsgate Without – its grim 400-foot (120m) long premises housing hundreds of paupers of all ages, survived into the 1830s. By the Victorian period, grandees like Sir Paul Pindar, whose splendid mansion was completed in 1600, had long ago vanished – his house had become a scruffy tavern and the surrounding streets and alleys, like those of nearby Spitalfields, were the resort of the urban poor. When cleared for the construction of Liverpool Street Station, the area contained 'some of the worst houses of their kind in London', some occupied by up to seven families living in squalor.[2] Plans for a comprehensive reconstruction of the area drawn up by George Dance the Younger as City Surveyor did not extend beyond the construction of Finsbury Circus, planned as a prestigious residential quarter – though Liverpool Street and Eldon Street, named after leading politicians of the day, were completed in 1829, providing a link from Moorgate to Bishopsgate.

The Victorian period saw the heart of the City transformed from a residential quarter to a global hub of finance and commerce with palatial banks, exchanges and insurance offices, but the parish of St Botolph Bishopsgate Without retained its character as a place of low-grade housing and small industries. All was to change with the coming of the railways. A great swathe of land was levelled for new stations and goods yards: this became the site of 1 Finsbury Avenue and Broadgate.

THE COMING OF THE RAILWAYS

THE COMING OF THE RAILWAYS

1 Finsbury Avenue – and subsequently Broadgate – was built on railway land, a large site developed from the 1860s onwards for passenger and freight traffic. Broad Street came first, before the adjoining Liverpool Street Station. By the 1970s, however, it was a sad sight: 'the saddest of all London stations', John Betjeman wrote, lamenting its 'fallen greatness'.[1] Today, the very existence of Broad Street, which in its heyday had handled half a million passengers weekly, is all but forgotten. The station, demolished in 1985, and its adjacent goods yard provided the site for the first phases of Broadgate (figs 2 & 4), a development that became the focus of the renewal of the City.

Railways, mainline and Underground, are fundamental to the very existence of the City of London as a financial and commercial hub: 120 million rail and Underground passengers pass annually through the mainline terminal and Underground station at Liverpool Street, London's third busiest terminal. The first railway to penetrate into the City was the London and Blackwall, opening a terminus at the Minories in 1840 and extending into Fenchurch Street a year later. In due course, Blackfriars, Holborn Viaduct and Cannon Street followed – all entering the City from the south across the Thames. By the mid-1860s, London's first underground railway, the Metropolitan, had extended as far as Moorgate (though it was not until 1876 that it reached Liverpool Street). The Eastern Counties Railway initially settled for a terminus just outside the City in shabby Shoreditch, opened in 1840 – it was optimistically renamed Bishopsgate a few years later, but a contemporary news report commented that 'not even the change of name from Shoreditch to Bishopsgate has ever made it a whit more attractive'.[2] By the 1860s, with the Eastern Counties amalgamated into the Great Eastern Railway and its lines extending the breadth of East Anglia, the decision was made to construct a new terminus within the City; however, it was more than a decade before the new Liverpool Street Station opened. The old Bishopsgate Station was rebuilt as a goods depot. (It survived until 1964, when it was destroyed by fire.)

Broad Street Station

Broad Street Station opened in November 1865, as the terminus of the North London Railway. Although it became one of the capital's busiest passenger carriers, the North London – initially known as the East & West India Docks and Birmingham Junction Railway – originated in plans for a route to connect the line from Birmingham (soon absorbed into the London & North Western Railway – the LNWR) with London's docks via a spur running through Hackney and Bow to Poplar. Although the transportation of freight was the original rationale for the line, passenger numbers grew rapidly to over 6.5 million in 1861. At first, North London Railway passengers were deposited at Fenchurch Street. However, with the backing of the LNWR – the majority shareholder in the North London – £1.2 million was spent on a 2-mile (3.2km) extension carried on viaducts at high level from Dalston to Broad Street, where the LNWR constructed a two-level goods depot adjacent to the new passenger terminal – both squeezed into a 2.5-acre (1ha) site. The latter – designed by William Baker, Chief Engineer to the LNWR – was described as being of 'mixed Italian style'. Betjeman called it an example of 'the best Town Hall style', though Alan Jackson thought it 'really rather horrid'.[3]

Serving what became the busiest suburban railway north of the Thames, with over 700 trains a day leaving and departing Broad Street, were a series of passenger stations described by Betjeman as 'minor Broad Streets, with billiard halls, vast booking halls and arcades of shops'.[4] Bow Station, particularly grand, featured a concert hall – intended to provide entertainment for

FIG.2
Broad Street Station in the 19th century.

FIG.3
Bishopsgate in 1837, before the coming of the railways.

FIG.4
Broad Street Station before closure.

North London employees, but later leased out as 'The Bow Palais' dance hall. Between 1910 and 1915, the LNWR ran a daily express restaurant-car service from Broad Street to Birmingham. The service was discontinued soon after the outbreak of war in 1914. By the early years of the twentieth century, however, the North London Railway was in decline, with its East End passenger base increasingly transferring to the Underground and to trams and buses. Second World War bombing wrecked most of the stations between Broad Street and Poplar, and passenger services were withdrawn completely in 1944. The western section of the North London system, running via Hampstead to Richmond, had been electrified in 1916 and continued to operate almost up to the closure of Broad Street, surviving the threat of the 'Beeching axe'. (It was later incorporated into the London Overground, which has also revived much of the East London route.) A service to Watford Junction also remained in operation to the end, but, post-war, there was the potential for a large swathe of land on the edge of the city to find a new use.

Following nationalisation in 1948, the new British Railways clearly saw Broad Street as an encumbrance. Passenger facilities were reduced to two cabins standing on the concourse, and in 1967–8 most of the remaining train-shed roofs, damaged by wartime bombs, were demolished. John Gay's evocative photographs, taken for Betjeman's 1972 book *London's Historic Railway Stations*, show the melancholy state of the once-busy station. The goods depot was closed in the 1960s, though the vast warehouse on the narrow side street of Finsbury Avenue survived – the remainder of the cleared site was let as a car park. By the 1970s, British Rail's Property Board was pursuing an increasingly aggressive approach to the profitable realisation of its assets, and historic buildings could not stand in its way. The fate of

FIG.5
Broad Street Station in the 19th century.

Broad Street had become inseparably linked to that of adjacent Liverpool Street.

Liverpool Street Station

Liverpool Street Station had been a long time in gestation, largely on account of funding issues. Proposals for a station located in Finsbury Circus, accessed by a series of viaducts, were thwarted by local opposition. The principle of a new station on the present site, approached at low level through cuttings and tunnels, won parliamentary approval in 1864. Lord Claud Hamilton, later Chairman of the Great Eastern Railway, declared it to be 'built on faulty principles, for it ought to have been constructed at street level'.[5] It was a decade before the first section of the station opened. The project, once launched, was completed at a cost of around £2 million in just two years, with the station fully opened in November 1875. Around 450 houses were cleared for its construction, displacing roughly 7000 people along with a gasworks and a theatre. This was essentially an engineering project, run by the Great Eastern's Chief Engineer, Edmund Wilson. The train sheds were magnificent – 'cathedralesque' was a fair description of the complex of what were essentially naves, aisles and transepts – but the architecture, simplified Gothic, was unremarkable, hardly rivalling that of George Gilbert Scott's Midland Hotel at St Pancras. From the start, Liverpool Street was, in effect, two stations – with suburban platforms, 550ft (170m) long, clustered to the west and mainline departure and arrival platforms, twice as long and extending almost to Liverpool Street, to the east, served by a cab road and with their own booking office. Wilson had been asked to provide for a possible station hotel – a feature of every major London terminal – but nothing was done until 1879 when Sir Charles Barry, architect of the Palace of Westminster, with his son, Charles Barry Junior, was commissioned to design what became the Great Eastern

FIG.6
The Great Eastern Hotel,
Liverpool Street Station.

Hotel (fig.6). Opened in 1884, it was split in two at street level by the station cab road. A major extension, designed by Colonel R.W. Edis (a weekend soldier and commanding officer, in succession to Lord Leighton, of the Artists' Rifles volunteers from 1883), was completed in 1901.

The hotel provided a comfortable retreat for affluent visitors from the shires but most of the passengers using the station were far from wealthy. Dedicated 'workmen's trains' were a speciality of the Great Eastern – the first arrived at 5.25 am. Cheap trains for better-paid workers arrived from 7 am onwards, bringing thousands of commuters from rapidly growing suburbs such as Leyton, Walthamstow and Ilford. The Great Eastern acquired the reputation of 'the poor man's line'; Liverpool Street was 'the people's station'. Booming passenger numbers created intolerable congestion, and the solution was

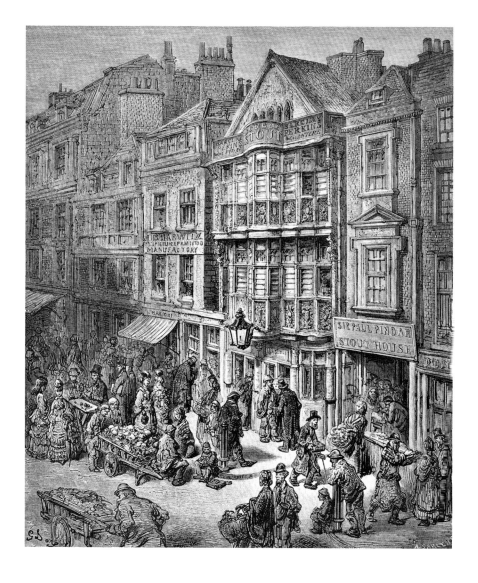

FIG.7
Drawing of the Pindar Mansion, Bishopsgate.

the construction in 1892–4 of eight more platforms on the eastern side of the station within a shed, structurally more matter-of-fact than its 1870s' predecessor, the project being overseen by W.N. Ashbee, Chief Architect to the Great Eastern. More of the urban poor were displaced, though this time the company reluctantly accepted the responsibility for rehousing them. Amongst the buildings on Bishopsgate facing demolition was a remarkable survivor: Sir Paul Pindar's seventeenth-century mansion, long used as a pub (fig.7). Pressure from antiquarians led to its being carefully dismantled, and the elaborate façade and some internal features were presented to the Victoria and Albert Museum.

The completion of the 1890s' extension made Liverpool Street a more disjointed station than ever – a long footbridge was now the principal means of access from west to east. Attached to it were three tearooms. One survived into the 1970s and delighted Betjeman, who considered Liverpool Street 'the most picturesque and interesting of the London termini' and knew 'no greater pleasure for elevenses in London than to sit in this teaplace and watch the trains arrive and depart'.[6] The architecture critic Ian Nairn warmed to 'its unplanned variety… the fey convolutions of the plan'.[7] The station suffered bomb damage in both world wars. In 1944, the left-wing journalist (and subsequently Labour MP) Tom Driberg wrote, 'is there any other London terminus so almost completely squalid, so tiringly chaotic, so true a type of the industrial capitalism which produced it?'[8] The post-war years saw few changes to the station. With Euston rebuilt in dismal fashion, British Rail turned its attention to Liverpool Street and Broad Street. The stage was set for a classic conservation battle – one in which Betjeman was sure to play a prominent part.

PLANNING BATTLES

PLANNING BATTLES

By the 1950s, London's great rail termini were shabby places, clearly in need of a major programme of investment and renewal. Most had survived the Second World War relatively unscathed, but by the late 1950s London was experiencing the beginnings of a property boom. British Railways (truncated to 'British Rail' in 1965) had come into existence in 1948 with nationalisation. Liverpool Street and Broad Street stations were now absorbed into BR's Eastern Region. With developers already transforming central London, the big stations had obvious potential for profitable redevelopment. The British Transport Commission – the central government body that controlled British Railways – was, however, legally prevented from developing its own property for anything but operational purposes. Everything changed in 1962, when the Transport Act opened the way for railway land to be profitably developed. A number of office schemes – at Waterloo, Cannon Street and Holborn Viaduct – were approved and begun before the newly elected Labour Government, with George Brown at the Department of Economic Affairs, imposed a ban on office development in central London in 1964. Some 43 potential developments on railway land were halted. The reconstruction of Euston, the first entirely new station built in London since Waterloo, began in 1962, but the office towers planned to sit above the station were vetoed. The new station opened in 1968.[1]

Euston and St Pancras

The construction of the new Euston had involved the destruction of the splendid Great Hall and the 'Arch' (fig.8; more correctly, a propylaeum) that fronted the station. The best efforts of the Victorian Society and luminaries such as John Betjeman failed to prevent what has since been recognised as a disastrous act of destruction. Next on BR's target list was St Pancras, where the former Midland Grand Hotel, the work of Sir

FIG.8
The Euston Arch.

FIG.9
St Pancras Hotel.

FIGS 10 & 11
Unbuilt Fizroy Robinson schemes for the redevelopment of Liverpool Street Station (from the 1991 book by Nick Derbyshire, *Liverpool Street: A Station for the Twenty-first century*).

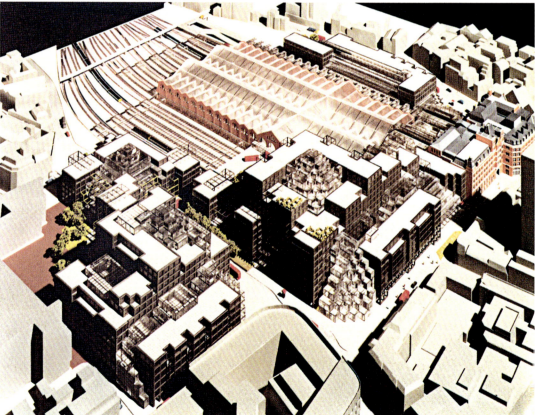

George Gilbert Scott, had been closed since 1935 and converted to railway offices. In 1967, plans for a possible closure of the station were made public – they had been first mooted in the 1930s, when there were already plans for rebuilding Euston and diverting trains from St Pancras into an enlarged station. But in the same year, thanks to Lord Kennet, then a junior government minister, St Pancras Station and the hotel were listed at Grade I, ruling out any scheme involving demolition (and opening the way for the eventual rebirth of the station as the terminus for Eurostar and the renaissance of the Midland Grand as a 5-star hotel).[2]

By the mid-1960s, BR had resolved to redevelop Liverpool Street, but the 'Brown Ban' on office development in central London made any progress with the scheme impossible. With the ban lifted, it became a practical possibility – but by 1973, the world economy was in recession. Plans were finally made public in 1975, on the basis of an Office Development Permit issued the previous year. Working in partnership with the big contractors Wimpey and Taylor Woodrow, BR's Property Board commissioned architects Fitzroy Robinson & Partners, a practice that had built extensively in the City, to develop a scheme providing for an entirely new station funded by office development. A series of office slabs, containing 1.2 million sq.ft (112,000 sq.m) of office space, would sit on a massive concrete raft over the tracks. The new station, with 22 platforms, would extend across the site of Broad Street Station, which was to be closed and demolished. The proposals quickly generated fierce opposition from a conservation lobby still lamenting the loss of Euston but heartened by the rescue of St Pancras. The conservationists had a powerful ally in the Labour-controlled Greater London Council (GLC), which resolved to oppose the scheme. Their case was strengthened by the Grade II listing, in August 1975, of the western train shed along with the L-shaped office building fronting the station and known as 50 Liverpool Street. (The Great Eastern Hotel was not listed until as late as 1993.)

Liverpool Street and Broad Street

Battle lines were drawn. A Liverpool Street Station Campaign (LISSCA) group was formed to spearhead opposition to BR's plans, with Poet Laureate (and passionate lover of railways) Sir John Betjeman as its President supported by a committee that included the comedian and author Spike Milligan and several MPs. LISSCA sought the retention of the entire station, while supporting a sensitive programme of improvements. The GLC was prepared to see substantial redevelopment; its sticking point was the retention of the western shed, which, it argued, merited Grade I listing and 'lay in the first rank of railway monuments'.[3] It was prepared to sacrifice 50 Liverpool Street. A public inquiry held between November 1976 and February 1977 considered both the principle of redeveloping Liverpool

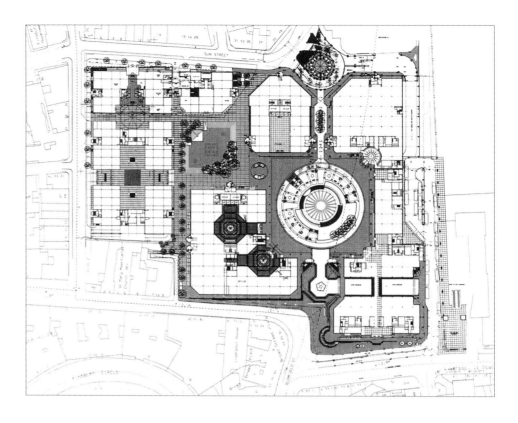

FIG.12
The Arup development scheme for Liverpool Street Station (from the 1991 book by Nick Derbyshire, *Liverpool Street: A Station for the Twenty-first Century*).

Street and Broad Street, with the associated commercial development, and the demolition of its listed elements. BR was adamant that it 'had no money with which to tart up relics of antiquity' and considered the western shed to be 'of marginal quality'.[4] The eminent architect Sir Hugh Casson, newly elected President of the Royal Academy, was recruited as a witness for BR, though even he felt that the western shed should be saved if it could be incorporated into the development plans. The City was determined to see the total redevelopment of a 'chaotic and murky station'. It was 1979 before the inquiry decision was published. Outline planning consent was given for the redevelopment of Liverpool Street and Broad Street, and the demolition of 50 Liverpool Street was permitted. However, the western shed had to be retained – an outcome that BR had effectively accepted after negotiations with the GLC – though it could be cut back at its southern end to accommodate a new station concourse.

Following the inquiry, BR carried out repairs to the western shed – a rather skimped project, with plastic replacing Victorian glazing in the roofs. Fitzroy Robinson revised its scheme to accommodate the western shed, providing a concourse awkwardly enclosed by offices with more development proposed on the southern part of the Broad Street site. By 1981, BR had resolved to separate the development of Liverpool Street from that of Broad Street. The way was opened for an inspired scheme, developed by Nick Derbyshire of BR's architecture and design group, with some input from writer and conservationist Simon Jenkins (a member of the BR Board from 1979), which extended the western shed to form a lofty new concourse incorporating a gallery with shops. 50 Liverpool Street was radically remodelled to create an impressive entrance to the station.[5]

FIG.13
The development scheme for Liverpool Street Station (from the 1991 book by Nick Derbyshire, *Liverpool Street: A Station for the Twenty-first Century*).

FIG.14
The western shed at Liverpool Street Station.

The planning impact of 1 Finsbury Avenue

The potential for placing all the 1.2 million sq.ft of commercial space consented in 1979 on the Broad Street site was highlighted by the success of 1 Finsbury Avenue, completed in 1984. Two schemes – by Fitzroy Robinson with funders Norwich Union, and Rosehaugh Stanhope Developments – were shortlisted. BR's decision to appoint the latter as its development partner undoubtedly owed much to the expertise offered by the architect and developer of 1 Finsbury Avenue, respectively, Peter Foggo and Stuart Lipton – the latter now in partnership with Godfrey Bradman. Moreover, the Finsbury Avenue scheme had been successfully negotiated with Hackney Council – and the site for what became Broadgate then lay mostly in Hackney. Broad Street Station, however, had still to be closed and demolished, and English Heritage recommended that it be listed.[6] The recommendation was rejected by the

FIG.15
Liverpool Street Station concourse today.

FIG.16
The cover of the 'SAVE Broad Street' report.

Minister, and a last-ditch campaign was launched by SAVE Britain's Heritage, with input from Arup engineers, arguing that the main station building, with the tracks and platforms gone, could be converted to shops and restaurants. In *SAVE Broad Street: a new use for the station building* (fig.16) published in May 1982, the group argued that 'the Broad Street forebuilding is capable of stunning transformation… The station forebuilding readily lends itself to a new use'. The campaign failed to halt demolition, which began in summer 1985. Construction of other blocks forming phases 1 and 2 of Broadgate was already under way on the goods-yard site, and 100 Liverpool Street, forming phase 3 of the development, was completed in the autumn of 1987 on the site of Broad Street Station, which was erased forever from the face of London.

CLIENT AND ARCHITECT

CLIENT AND ARCHITECT

1 Finsbury Avenue was a project that pioneered new strategies for procuring, designing and constructing commercial buildings in Britain. It was the product of an alliance between two radical thinkers, the architect Peter Foggo (1930–93) and the developer Stuart Lipton (b.1942). (figs 17 and 18) The present owners, British Land and GIC, together with their architects, Allford Hall Monaghan Morris (AHMM), have applied their own innovative thinking, in what is essentially a dynamic reimagining of the building in tune with the London of the twenty-first century.

Sir Stuart Lipton – he was knighted in 2000 – emerged as a significant player on the London development scene in the 1970s. In partnership with Geoffrey Wilson, firstly at Sterling Land and subsequently (from 1976) Greycoat, he completed major office developments in Hammersmith, Euston and Victoria. In 1978, a

FIG.17
Peter Foggo (right) on the original 1FA construction site, with Director of Laing Management, Paul Weller.

FIG.18
Interior of Gun Wharf, Chatham
– the Corporation of Lloyd's
administrative headquarters –
by Arup Associates.

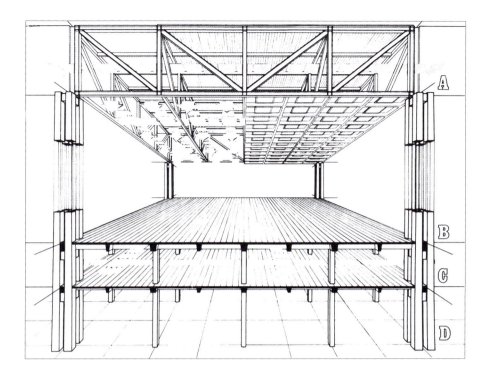

FIGS.19 & 20:
Left: Gun Wharf, Chatham, by Arup Associates.
Right: Horizon Factory plan.

consortium of the Standard Life Company and Greycoat acquired a complex of historic Georgian warehouses at Cutler Street, on the eastern edge of the City of London. A mix of radical conversion, with original interiors gutted, and redevelopment produced Cutlers Gardens, completed in 1982 and a commercial success despite its location on what was then seen as the City fringe. (It was actually a short walk from Bishopsgate.) In some respects, this development, with its generous provision of public space, prefigured Broadgate.[1] Greycoat's architect at Cutlers Gardens was the practice of Richard Seifert & Partners. Headed by Richard Seifert (1910–2001), the firm was a dominant presence on the commercial-development scene throughout the 1960s and 70s. Other practices commissioned by Greycoat included Renton Howard Wood Levin (RHWL) and Elsom Pack Roberts (EPR). Like Seifert & Partners, they were unashamedly 'commercial' and their work often received short shrift from architectural critics.

Critically approved practices, in contrast, typically eschewed commissions from developers and thrived on work for the public sector: schools, universities, social housing and hospitals.

Arup Associates – and Peter Foggo

The practice of Arup Associates fell into this latter category.[2] It had been established in 1963 after a decade as a 'building group' within the engineering practice of Ove Arup & Partners, with Philip Dowson, Bob Hobbs and Derek Sugden as founding partners. Its earliest projects were innovative factories for new-style industries, mostly located in the New Towns established after the Second World War, but by the 1960s it was working on a string of university projects at Oxford, Cambridge, Birmingham, Loughborough and Leicester. Peter Foggo (fig.17) – born in 1930 in Liverpool, the son of a watchmaker – joined Arup in 1959, after a short stint working for Architects' Co-

FIG.21:
Horizon Factory.

FIGS. 22 & 23:
Horizon Factory plans.

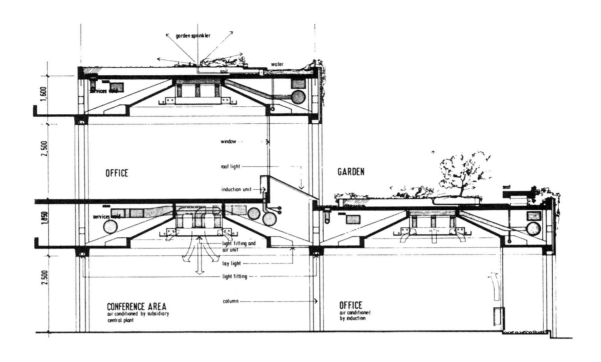

Partnership. (He continued to work with David Thomas, another Arup recruit who had joined the Building Group in 1958, on a series of outstanding private houses, of which the Sorrell House in Sussex, completed in 1960, is the finest.) Foggo became a partner in Arup Associates in 1966. The practice was innovative in its multidisciplinary organisation, with architects, engineers and other professionals working together in groups. Foggo headed up Group 2, running it, Stuart Lipton recalled, as 'virtually an independent practice'.[3] The group was known for its democratic ethos: Foggo, unlike other Arup partners, refused to have a private office and sat with the other architects. In 1968, Group 2, established a few years earlier to work on major projects for Loughborough University, began work on the largest project yet undertaken by Arup Associates, a 1.3 million sq.ft (125,000 sq.m) factory for tobacco manufacturers Players in Nottingham. Following a year or more of site clearance – the site had been used as a rubbish dump and was heavily polluted – the Horizon Factory was completed in 1971 to a fast-track construction strategy, using repetitive components, on the basis of a management contract operated by Bovis Ltd, under which 'its architects worked inside the design team instead of following the ancient tradition of trying to lead it from over the horizon'.[4]

Management contracts with Bovis were again used for two large office projects for paper manufacturers Wiggins Teape in Basingstoke. Gateway 1, housing 1000 staff relocated from London, was completed in 1976. Influenced by Herman Hertzberger's Centraal Beheer (completed in 1972), which Foggo and his team visited, it was, like 1 Finsbury Avenue, listed in 2015. A few years later, Wiggins Teape commissioned a second building, Gateway 2, on an adjacent site, completed in 1982 following an 18-month construction schedule. Unlike its air-conditioned neighbour, Gateway 2 was naturally

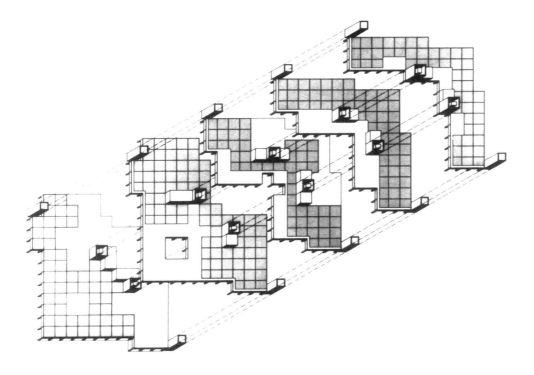

ventilated and a notable feature was a full-height central atrium, constructed on a steel frame and channelling daylight into office spaces. Its relationship to the atrium at 1 Finsbury Avenue is clear. Indeed, Gateway 2, into which Wiggins Teape transferred its headquarters within a few years, pointed the way towards a new generation of office buildings. The *Architects' Journal* commented on the spectacular atrium that:

> invested as it is with a rich diversity of activities, it helps to show that the reductivist approach, which in so many buildings insisted upon a firm division of *served* and *servant* spaces, was often an extravagance and an irrelevance. The purpose of technology in architecture should be to serve human needs at all levels. If this can be achieved simply and economically, it must be preferable to a display of mere machinery.[5]

The completion of Gateway 2 came at a time when Lipton was reconsidering his architectural commissioning strategy – it led him to conclude that 'the institutional architects were actually more commercial than those known for commercial practice'.[6]

A friend – the distinguished engineer, and Arup partner, Jack Zunz (1923–2018) – introduced Lipton to Philip Dowson at Arup Associates, and he was taken to see the prestigious bespoke offices that the practice had recently completed for the Central Electricity Generating Board (CEGB) in Bristol and for Lloyd's of London in Chatham. The quality of the architecture 'came as a revelation… it was my conversion', Lipton recalled.[7] He was particularly impressed by the atrium at Gateway 2. He wrote to Philip Dowson following these visits, and Dowson replied on 24 March 1981: 'In general, I think there is no doubt that we are both aiming for the same end – excellence architecture in commercial buildings.'

FIGS. 24–27:
Exterior of Gateway 1; interior of Gateway 2. Wiggins Teape.

Dowson continued, 'in the present state of flux we must agree that the best way of achieving this is an open subject. The relationship between the designer and client, designer and contractor, and the client and contractor needs reassessment'. Addressing the changing nature of the development industry, Dowson wrote, 'we would welcome any steps which would involve the industry to a greater extent and which, at the same time, did not put at risk your own interests or the quality of the design'. A management contract – 'still a developing art' – might be the best way forward, Dowson suggested.[8]

With 1 Finsbury Avenue in active planning, Lipton met with Peter Foggo – whom, in fact, he had known for several years at Arup Associates' Soho office. Foggo presented a number of possible designs for the site. The one that was selected closely resembled what was built. Lipton recalled their first meeting on the project:

Eight simple drawings showing the analysis of the building options were presented. No architecture, just block plans showing the massing impact on the environment and public spaces. Peter's logical, calm description of the alternatives had every step worked out, with Peter (as I was to learn) always a step ahead… He was one of the first quality architects to break the mould of what might be called rent slab architecture. Peter's big floor-plate strategy not only produced spaces that the consumer needed, but a building form which related to the street.

For Lipton, Foggo 'helped me to bridge the gap between institutional and commercial architecture'.[9]

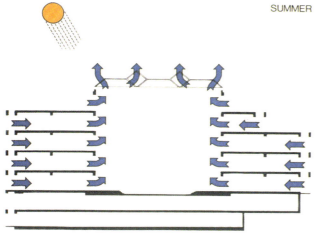
SUMMER

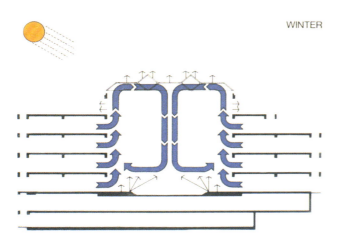
WINTER

FIG.28:
Wiggins Teape, Gateway 2.

DESIGNING
1 FINSBURY AVENUE

DESIGNING 1 FINSBURY AVENUE

Greycoat's experience at Cutlers Gardens was that the larger floors let first. Stuart Lipton recalls, 'the market wanted big floors. We knew from the USA that big floors were the coming thing, but the norm in Britain was 45ft (14m) deep office floors'.[1] At 1 Finsbury Avenue, the atrium was an important element in a design strategy that provided for 32,000 sq.ft (3000 sq.m) office floors 60ft (18m) deep. (In contrast, Seifert's NatWest Tower, completed in 1981, featured floors of around 10,000 sq.ft [930 sq.m]), and those were disposed around a massive central service/lift core.) The atrium provided a source of natural light for these large floors, but for Foggo, who greatly admired Charles Barry's atrium in London's Reform Club, it had other benefits. 'The average office space the world over is dull', he wrote in 1985, continuing:

> it's a 'one note' building. Using an atrium in an office building at least helps you to start the spatial experience higher up the scale… The atrium can be a glorious space – its glory is its most powerful advantage – and having got it, it should be exploited for its virtues. It is functionally beautiful to have a well-designed atrium to look into; it can also be a lobby, a circulation space, and a space for all kinds of activities. But what really matters is the *space*.[2]

Developing the design

With the basic diagram of 1 Finsbury Avenue established – deep plan, medium rise (eight storeys, plus basement) – Foggo's Group 2 worked on developing the designs (figs 29–32). The team, most of whom had worked on the two Gateway projects, included architects Rab Bennetts, Ian Taylor and Bill Malcolmson, engineers Peter Skead and Tony Taylor, quantity surveyor Bruce Vickers and design manager/administrator Les Winter. The fundamental issue on which Foggo and Lipton disagreed related to the structure of the building. Foggo

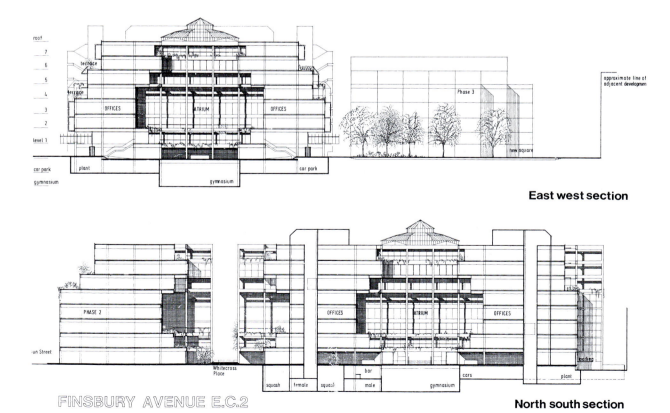

East west section

North south section

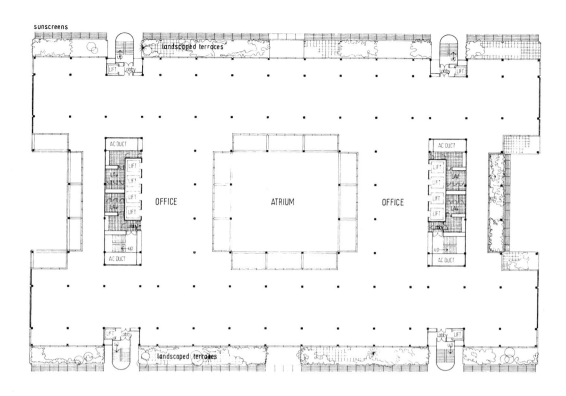

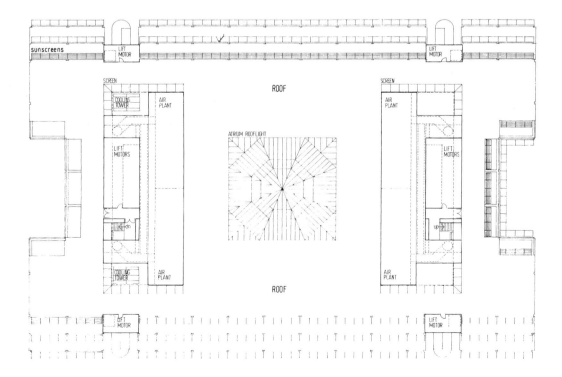

FIGS. 29–31:
1 Finsbury Avenue original design drawings.

FIG.32:
1 Finsbury Avenue original design drawings.

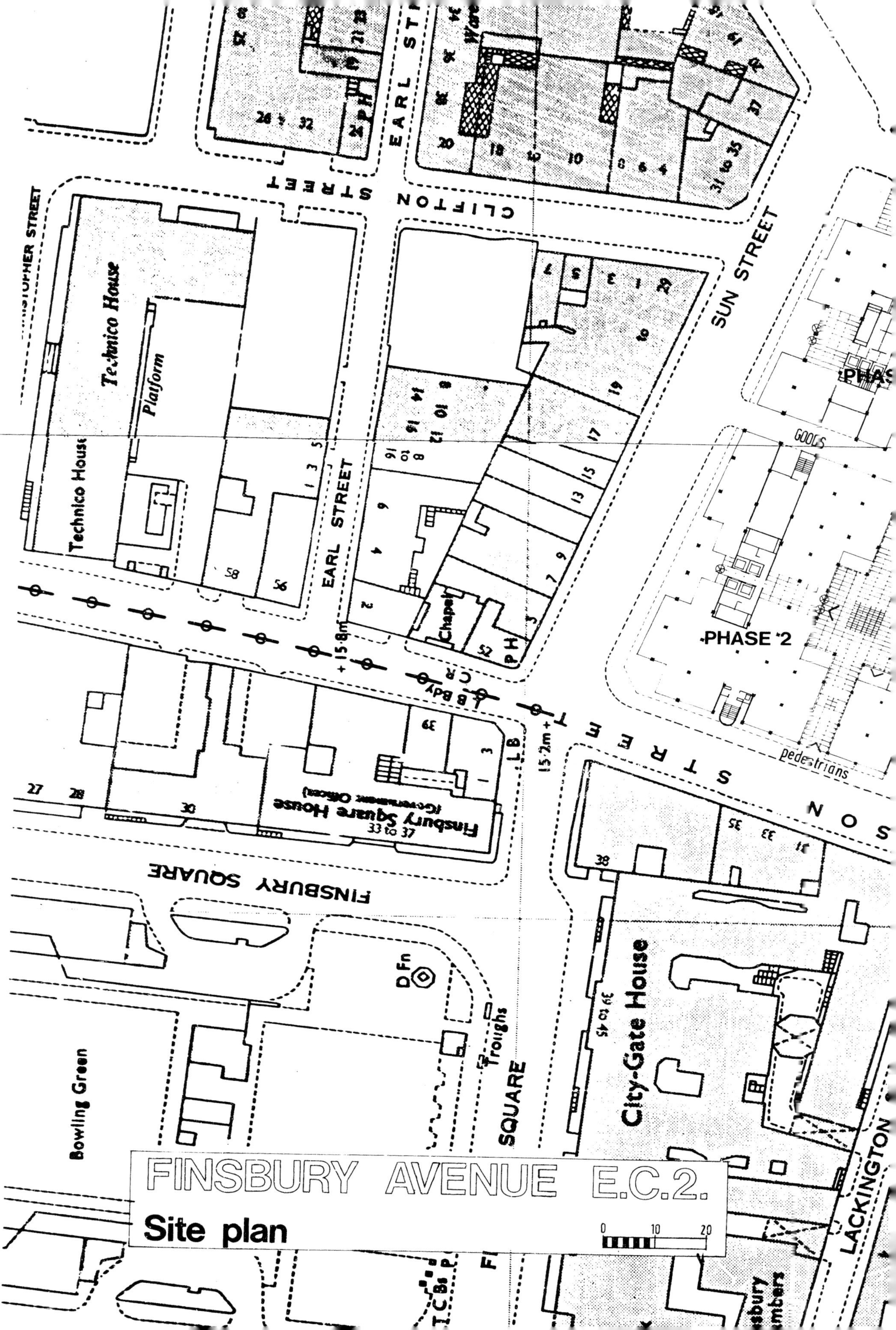

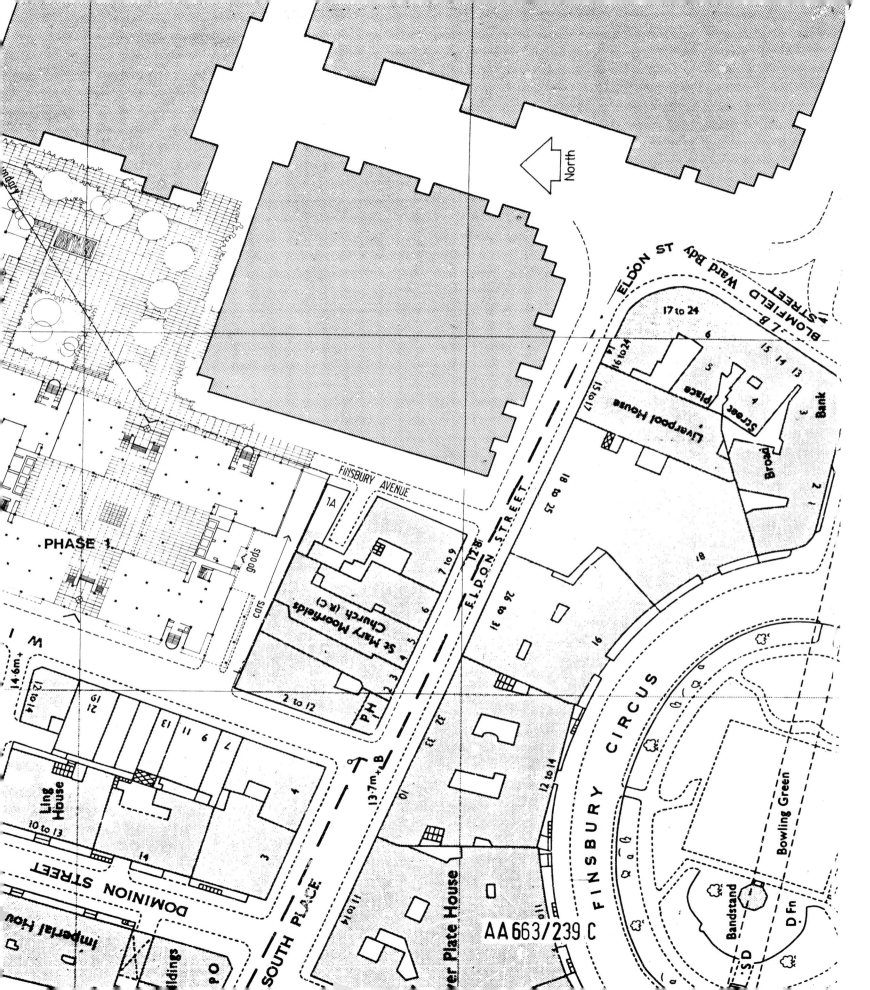

FIG.33:
The Reform Club atrium –
drawing from the 19th century.

was intent on using an internally exposed concrete structure, featuring a vaulted slab – with ducts between the voids – that was a development of that used in the Gateway projects. Lipton, influenced by American fast-track models, was determined to use steel. To convince Foggo and team that the USA had all the answers, Lipton arranged for 14 members of Group 2 to travel to New York and Chicago in early 1982, visit projects, and meet leading architects including Bruce Graham of Skidmore, Owings and Merrill (SOM) and Kevin Roche. SOM had recently completed Chicago's Sears Tower, and was working on its competition entry for an extension to the National Gallery in London (Arup Associates was, by chance, another contender for the project). Rab Bennetts recalled that:

we returned to London unimpressed by what we had seen and heard. Not only had the design teams

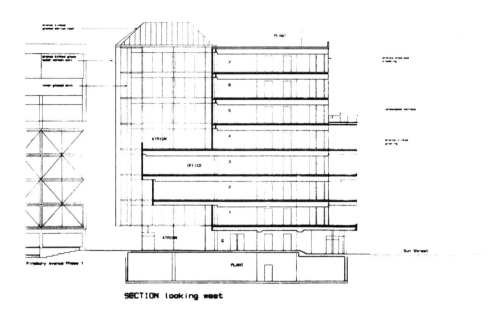

FIG.34:
1 Finsbury Avenue – Phase 1 construction section.

been supplanted by construction managers taking the leading decisions, the quality of construction was also lower than what we had expected except for finishes in areas such as the office lobbies. We tactfully declined Stuart Lipton's invitation to make a presentation of our findings …[3]

Ian Taylor – who had joined Arup in 1981, working on the Liverpool Garden Festival pavilion with Richard Frewer – recalls that there was a core belief at Arup Associates that structure and architecture were inseparable, and steel construction was unfamiliar territory there. Nonetheless, steel, Lipton insisted, was to be the raw material for 1 Finsbury Avenue, generating neutral internal spaces to be colonised by tenants. There was pressure on the architects to make the steel frame as economical as possible. The building was an envelope ready to be customised – the architecture was to be

FIG.35
1 Finsbury Avenue looking south along Wilson Street.

found largely in the design of the atrium and façades. 'We put a lot of effort into the design of the cladding', Taylor recalls. 'It defined the building and we worked intensively on it with Hans Siedentopf of Gartners'.[4] (The Bavarian company Josef Gartner GmbH was pre-eminent in the design and installation of cladding systems.) Siedentopf was an extraordinary figure – a hardened chain-smoker who quickly established a remarkably fruitful working relationship with Foggo and his team and made a major contribution to the design of 1 Finsbury Avenue.

The client's insistence on steel construction had been a major issue for Foggo. Rab Bennetts recalls that 'Peter was disconsolate and for a moment it seemed likely he would resign'. This was, as Foggo saw it, essentially an instruction to abandon the idea of a truly integrated building, in which the structure determined the spatial order of the architecture. The sequence of buildings that began with Loughborough and developed on a heroic scale with the Players Factory, culminating with the two Wiggins Teape buildings, was at an end. The notion of a neutral interior also threatened the multidisciplinary nature of Arup Associates, as 'the engineers' contribution was suppressed within the architecture'. The client and architect seemed to be irretrievably at odds. However, Foggo 'picked himself up and immersed himself in the two areas that were not compromised by Lipton's decision – the façade and the atrium'.[5] The final designs for the façade as a double-height repetitive module were developed by Foggo, who drew dozens of possible variants before arriving at the version that was built. The chosen design, developed in consultation with Gartners, had an affinity with the work of Mies van der Rohe – there are echoes here of the Barcelona Pavilion and the IIT campus in Chicago.

Once the matter of the basic material of the building had been resolved, Foggo and Lipton quickly established an amicable working relationship as the former threw himself into the project. Writing after Foggo's death, Stuart Lipton remembered him as 'always patient, stretching, searching, demanding, and when you see something his way, his determination showed the way forward'. Key decisions were taken at meetings between the two in the early morning and on Sundays: 'With just a drawing we would speedily make decisions, no notes, no doubts, Risks yes, but always innovation and care'.[6] Detailed matters were left to the team meetings that took place every Tuesday. The same highly productive working relationship went on to power the Broadgate development.

Planning and letting issues
The site at Finsbury Avenue – the former railway warehouse, now owned by National Carriers Ltd – had first been identified by Godfrey Bradman of Rosehaugh as having development potential. Rosehaugh was a 'shell entity', an old tea-broking business that had been taken over by Bradman as a tool for his property finance and development ventures. Bradman approached Greycoat, inviting it to acquire a 50 per cent stake in its redevelopment as offices. Greycoat was a 'merchant developer', light on assets and dependent on finance from lenders. Lipton and Bradman formed a potent alliance – they were soon to embark on Broadgate (as Rosehaugh Stanhope), again with Arup Associates, after Lipton had left Greycoat (before 1 Finsbury Avenue was completed). For 1 Finsbury Avenue, however, it was Greycoat's successful record as a developer that persuaded other investors – including Globe Investment; Jacob Rothschild; and, most significantly, British Land (then led by its Chairman, John Ritblat) – to sink funds – a total of £34 million – into a project that seemed to some risky, given its location outside the City boundary and within the London Borough of Hackney. Moreover, Arup Associates was a newcomer to the world of speculative office development. To Ritblat, however, it

FIG.36
Finsbury Avenue Square.

FIG.37
1 Finsbury Avenue,
Wilson Street view.

was 'a good punt. Arups had a good scheme that was relatively cheap. It was in a fringe area, effectively down and out, but the potential was obvious'. British Land was eventually to assume full ownership of what became Broadgate in 1996.[7] Since 2013, the estate has been owned by a partnership of British Land and Singapore-based GIC, forming a joint venture to spearhead the renewal of Broadgate.

'The letting agents thought the building was too big', Lipton says. 'They reckoned a rent of £14 per sq.ft was the most we'd get. We were counting on £18.50 – and got it'.[8] With the funding secured, work could start on site at the end of 1982. To construct the building, Rosehaugh Greycoat went to Laings, a contractor with whom it had already worked on several projects, and a management contract similar to that used for Arup Associates' Basingstoke projects, but specially drafted by property lawyer Ann Minogue, was agreed.

The planning process had been potentially tricky, given Labour-controlled Hackney Council's known aversion to developers. But there were attractions for the local authority in the scheme: the prospect of lucrative business rates should office developers colonise this corner of the borough – plus planning-gain benefits, which could be negotiated. Patrick Robinson, who worked on the planning process as assistant to Garry (later Lord) Hart of City law firm Herbert Smith & Co., recalls 'a *very* complex and sophisticated negotiation' with Hackney's lawyers. A Section 52 Agreement was negotiated with Hackney. 'The local politicians stayed well under the radar.'[9] This agreement covered all issues relating to the development: the developer's interests were represented by David Blackburn, a lawyer recently appointed a director of Rosehaugh, and Barry Cockerell, a property-management surveyor by background and by now a director of Greycoat. Greycoat was impressed by Hackney's chief planning officer, Ray Michael, who liked

Designing 1 Finsbury Avenue

FIG.38:
Finsbury Avenue Square.

FIG.39
1 and 2 Finsbury Avenue.

the scheme and did much to convince the leadership of the council to back it. The then-leader of the council opposed the plans; Ray Michael was able to win over the members. 'The planning was highly political', Patrick Robinson recalls. 'The easy sell was probably the Peter Foggo design, which was regarded as innovative, flexible, fresh, and of unquestionably high quality.'[10] For Hackney Council, whatever the reservations of some of its members, the scheme was seen as a gateway, pointing the way towards the expansion of high-value City developments within its boundaries.

One matter to be resolved was the closure of Finsbury Avenue, a very minor thoroughfare but a public street nonetheless. Even as 1 Finsbury Avenue was on site, plans were in place for numbers 2 and 3, with a new public square that would in a few years connect to Broadgate. They were completed in 1987–8, by which time all the Arup blocks at Broadgate had been completed by Rosehaugh Stanhope – Stuart Lipton having quit Greycoat in 1983 to establish Stanhope and form a renewed alliance with Godfrey Bradman. He continued as a major player on the development scene. Working in a new consortium, he began construction of Stockley Park, the pioneering business park near Heathrow Airport, in 1985, with Arup Associates again as architect. The list of projects with which Lipton has been associated is a long one, including the redevelopment of Paternoster Square and Ludgate in the City of London and the Central St Giles project in Westminster, designed by Renzo Piano. But he does not hesitate when asked which of his projects he takes most pride in – and it is 1 Finsbury Avenue.

BUILDING
1 FINSBURY AVENUE

BUILDING
1 FINSBURY AVENUE

Greycoat's agenda for 1 Finsbury Avenue was straightforward: a high-quality building delivered in record time. The construction-management procurement strategy was commonplace in the USA but virtually unknown in Britain. Its attraction was the degree of control it gave to the developer. Construction management was used with great success at Broadgate, but in 1982 it was a step too far. Arup Associates had a standard management contract, used in Peter Foggo's earlier projects, and this was adapted by construction lawyer Ann Minogue. The contract drawn up with Laings provided for completion within 18 months, with penalties for delays; in the event, the building was completed in 15 months. Laing's team was directed by Paul Lewis, trained as a civil engineer. 'It was a new way of doing things. Group 2 at Arups had all the talents – they provided an integrated service, brilliantly led by Foggo. He was inspirational, a designer with a clear grip on the construction process and able to take decisions on the spot.'[1]

The brief for 1 Finsbury Avenue had emerged from Greycoat's intensive study of American construction strategies. 'Greycoat's see construction as a total *interactive* process with client, design team and contractor thrashing problems out together… They know how buildings are put together and work; their brief calls for external walls designed on a grid with no random plant protrusions at roof level, and it forbids "fashion engineering" on the environmental services. But it is not just the end product that matters – so too does he process.'[2] The objective was maximising quality and speed, and procuring good-value construction. But, the *Architects' Journal* commented approvingly, 'Greycoat's are striving to perfect their product, establishing new standards and ensuring that all involved in the design, production and assembly of components into the

FIGS.40–43:
1 Finsbury Avenue under construction.

completed building attain those standards'.³ Peter Carolin, writing in the *AJ,* was enthused by the alliance of a developer with a prestigious architectural practice:

> all too often speculative office building in the UK takes the form of dreary buildings which display all the old easy solutions. The lowest common denominator prevails in the form (mansarditis) and the details (expenditure on surface ostentation rather than spatial and servicing efficiency). The occasional architectural vulgarities and their accompanying structural gymnastics are part of this way of doing things. But Finsbury Avenue is light years ahead. Arups give the impression of relishing the challenge and Greycoat's seem to approve.⁴

The construction strategy

Fundamental to the project was the concept of US-style 'shell and core' construction. Tenants were to be provided with office areas that were little more than structural shells, though suspended ceilings and raised floors were provided, leaving them to install fit-outs and servicing to suit their specific needs. The first tenants were to be offered a fitting-out allowance of £5 per sq.ft – a basic partitioning and servicing system designed by Arup was available for their use. More traditional approaches to the design of office buildings gave tenants fully fitted-out spaces – all too often, these were soon ripped out and refitted, resulting in added costs and delays. Letting the building as shell and core was thus advantageous to both developer and tenant. But it was seen as too radical by letting agents at 1 Finsbury Avenue and, to Stuart Lipton's dismay, was dropped. Lipton declared exasperatedly that 'the estate agents are really the source of this; and also, frankly, property companies haven't pushed it hard enough. Tenants had to spend money removing fit-out they did not want.'⁵ Lipton was soon vindicated: letting office space as

FIG.44:
1 Finsbury Avenue under construction.

FIGS 45–46:
1 Finsbury Avenue - interior construction drawings.

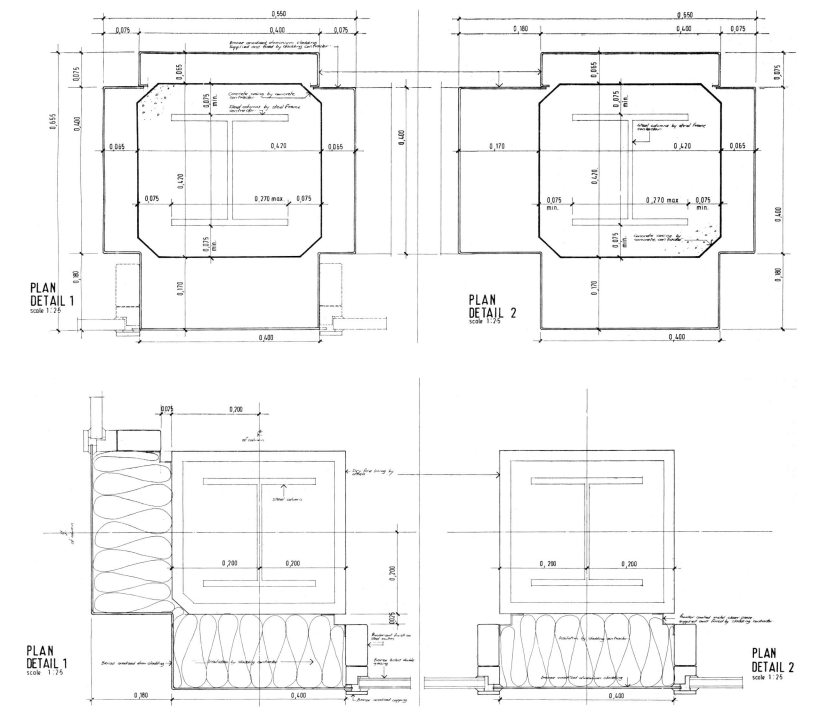

shell and core soon became standard practice in the speculative-office market, and was key to the success of Broadgate. Frank Duffy of the practice DEGW, a pioneer of radical new thinking about office design, had coined the phrase 'shell, services, scenery and sets', envisaging buildings and their component parts in terms of layers of longevity. A building should be designed, Duffy argued, to accommodate technological change and new working methods. The relevance of this thinking to a new world of globalised information technology and to a London about to be shaken by the impact of the 'Big Bang', the deregulation of London's financial markets that took place in 1985, was obvious, and DEGW was to have an important role in the development of Broadgate in tailoring buildings to the needs of future tenants.

Peter Foggo – resigned to the use of steel, rather than exposed concrete, as the basic component of the building – worked with his team to make a success of the construction strategy. Tony Taylor recalls, 'we presented the client with two schemes for the structure: a steel frame with a high quality precast floor structure exposed on the underside, incorporating air ducts, or a steel frame with a simple metal deck and composite floor slab'.[6] The latter was chosen for economy and speed of construction – Greycoat had, in fact, already used steel-frame construction for the Cutlers Court development, located opposite Cutlers Gardens and designed by RHWL. It was soon to become a commonplace feature of office buildings in Britain. Standard British practice, since steel construction became widespread at the end of the nineteenth century, was that steel must be encased in concrete and generally buried beneath brick or stone. Changes to London's stringent fire-proofing regulations, which had stipulated that steel frames be encased in masonry, made all-steel structures a highly economical proposition. At 1 Finsbury Avenue, protective boarding

FIGS.47–48:
1 Finsbury Avenue atrium.

FIG.49:
Lloyd's of London – Richard Rogers and Partners.

FIG.50:
Joseph Paxton's Crystal Palace.

was applied to the steel internally (with concrete casing for external steelwork). The raw material for the building was 1500 tons of rolled steel, using sections of simple rectilinear form with repetitive elements and simple bolted connections. The structural frame was erected in just 13 weeks. Floors were 5 inches (130mm) thick, with *in situ* concrete planks sitting on profiled steel sheeting. Suspended ceilings – which Foggo was reluctant to install – incorporated lighting and air conditioning. Staircases were fabricated off site and installed as the main frame was going up, so that they could be used by construction workers. Everything was kept simple, lean and designed for flexibility in use. The most striking internal feature was, of course, the full-height atrium, capped by a glazed octagonal dome. Securing consent for the atrium was far from straightforward and required extended negotiation with the fire officer. There was also the issue of finding a contractor capable of constructing it. Its form was inevitably reminiscent of the iron-and-glass conservatories of the Victorian period. The glazing bars were, however, not ornamental but structural. At first- and second-floor level, the atrium stepped back to provide galleries – though these were of little practical use.

Façade and atrium

1 Finsbury Avenue proved to be a very efficient commercial building, which had a major impact on the design of office buildings in Britain. As architecture, however, its impact was largely external. *The Buildings of England's* comments typified a highly positive critical reception – 'the whole is immensely refined, without mannerism or extravagant multiplication of motifs'.[7] The use of prefabricated components was an important element in its fast-track construction strategy, taking inspiration from nineteenth-century engineering projects such as the Crystal Palace (fig.50). 'High-tech' architects were drawn to this approach, and it featured in such prestigious projects as Norman Foster's Hong Kong and Shanghai Bank and Richard Rogers' Lloyd's of London (fig.49) – both on site in 1982, and both focused on the creation of flexible space. But both these buildings were highly expensive one-off, bespoke products (the Lloyd's project extended over nearly a decade from commission to completion). At 1 Finsbury Avenue, a similar approach was applied to the world of speculative office development and to a much more modest budget. The building was extremely efficient in its spatial design.

A key player in the project was the German cladding manufacturer Josef Gartner of Gundelfingen, near Munich. The company had supplied the bronze, anodised metal cladding for Foggo's Gateway 1 and Gateway 2 projects and an excellent working relationship developed with their team, led by Hans Siedentopf, with whom Peter Foggo worked closely on the curtain wall at 1 Finsbury Avenue. Siedentopf was, Stuart Lipton recalls, 'quite choosy about the projects he took on – we were fortunate to have him on board'.[8] Laings had worked with Siedentopf and respected his judgement. Gartners proposed a baked paint finish for the cladding. (Barry Cockerell of Greycoat expressed some concern at the use of aluminium – 'this particular material displayed unsatisfactory characteristics in the Royal Navy's recent experiences in the South Atlantic', he pointed out.)[9] There was brief flirtation with a silver finish, with a model made to show its effect – but bronze, as at Gateway 1, was the natural choice. 'We concluded that a street of that kind and scale could not take a loud, glittering façade', Foggo commented in the *Architects' Journal*.[10] Cladding sections, incorporating glazing, were assembled in multi-storey units and craned into place. Scaffolding was not needed. The window mullions and transoms contained a low-temperature hot-water heating system, already used by Gartners on a number of projects but still a relatively novel idea in Britain.

FIG.51
Level 4 office
before refurbishment.

FIG.52:
The inside of the listed façade from Level 7.

(It worked well, and has been retained as part of the refurbishment project completed by AHMM.)

The atrium apart, the architecture of 1 Finsbury Avenue was largely, and deliberately, external — indeed, the strongly modelled, layered façades, punctuated by landscaped terraces, were the feature that attracted particular critical acclaim. Sun screening was part of the environmental programme for the building — which was, in many respects, far from innovative. The substitution of steel for concrete as the raw material of the building had an impact on the designs — the benefits of using the thermal mass of concrete to absorb heat were lost. Natural ventilation, as used at Gateway 2 in Basingstoke, was simply not acceptable in the City market. The building's long east and west elevations featured sunscreens that also provided convenient access to the façades for maintenance and window cleaning. Diagonal

restraining bracing – which echoed that on Piano and Rogers' Pompidou Centre – strongly expressed escape stairs, and set-backs at first- and fourth-floor level (over entrances) further animated the façades. Ground-floor columns were clad in polished granite. 'Such materials have become the architectural equivalent of pinstripes and clearly denote up-market office', commented the *Architectural Review*, adding, 'The transition from bronze aluminium to granite seems scarcely worth the trouble'.[11] The granite cladding, using stone selected by Foggo in Italy, has been dispensed with in the recent refurbishment. The *AR* praised the façade treatment for its 'detail, depth and delicacy as well as a sense of human scale and some of the richness of the old buildings around'. It was unusual for the *Review*, the most esteemed architectural voice in Britain, to praise – or even review – a speculative office development. Yet it lauded 1 Finsbury Avenue as 'more than an exercise in shoe-horning in. The design goes to considerable lengths to achieve a striking identity and sense of generous calm within; and the building is the first phase of a planned new urban place – or rather a network of places'. The reviewer, Peter Buchanan, concluded that 'Arups have provided an object lesson for all architects. They prove that spec offices can make a sensitive contribution to a civic environment'.[12] Patrick Hannay, writing in the *Architects' Journal*, commented on the impact of the project on Arup Associates: 'ten years ago it would have been unthinkable that Arup Associates, then renowned for Oxford college buildings and vast, purpose-built public sector headquarters offices, should have sailed into the pole position in the spec office league table'.[13]

The constructional impact of 1 Finsbury Avenue

In many ways, 1 Finsbury Avenue provided lessons that informed Broadgate. The fast-track construction strategy was hugely successful – thanks to the use of steel as the basic material of the building, 'we built more quickly than the Americans', Tony Taylor recalls.[14] The 1 Finsbury Avenue project was a success in its own right, but equally it informed forthcoming projects and was a marker for change in the construction industry. 'I always believe that the start of building introduces a new wave of thought processes which liven up one's previous ideas or consolidate one's views', Lipton wrote to Foggo in December 1982.[15]

A comprehensive assessment of the building in use – the building was now largely occupied – appeared in the *Designers' Journal* in January 1985. It looked at the issue of how Arup Associates – accustomed to designing bespoke buildings for clients such as Lloyd's of London, IBM and the CEGB – responded to the very different world of speculative development. Externally, 1 Finsbury Avenue was 'unmistakably an Arup building… The image is utterly consistent'.[16] Internally, however, the fit-out commissioned by tenants varied dramatically in style. Stockbrokers Rowe & Pitman had installed plaster cornices, fabric wall covering, and a fake chimney breast with a neo-Victorian (fake) fireplace in their boardroom – 'the designers have gone all out to recreate the atmosphere of a gentlemen's club'.[17]

Marketing 1 Finsbury Avenue – then and now

What was indisputable was the market success of 1 Finsbury Avenue. 'The truth of Finsbury Avenue's success is that we never marketed it at all', Barry Cockerell of Greycoat revealed.[18] The appeal of the building extended beyond such remarkably astute (non-) marketing. Stuart Lipton saw the building as the outcome of a particularly fruitful relationship between developer and architect. 'We start off with a very clear brief to the architect, then he responds, and we look to him to take those steps further. I can't be an architect myself, I can't attempt to, but I can give him design freedoms and I

FIG.53:
Level 5 bolted column splices and glazing overlooking the Upper Atrium.

can hopefully set standards of excellence'.[19] At Finsbury Avenue, that formula created one of the outstanding commercial buildings of its age. For Chris Strickland, who joined the team as project manager in November 1982, 1 Finsbury Avenue was nothing less than the first of a new generation of buildings, not least because 'it was designed for change – the first of a new breed of buildings'.[20] It was this inherent flexibility that has ensured the building's continued success and fuelled its recent rebirth.

British Land's inspired reimagining of 1 Finsbury Avenue started with a clear recognition of the significance of the building. As Nigel Webb, the company's Head of Developments, comments, 'we recognised that 1 Finsbury Avenue is one of the jewels in the Broadgate crown and a truly outstanding and original building. We also recognised the significance of the building in Broadgate's history and its inherent quality, flexibility and adaptability.' For Webb, the building is nothing less than a modern classic: 'With a bit of reimagining we could see the building being a further catalyst for the delivery of our vision for Broadgate'.[21]

British Land's choice of Allford Hall Monaghan Morris as architects for the careful – but in some respects radical – reinvention of 1 Finsbury Avenue was a shrewd move. With its regard for history and dynamic approach to the reinvention of existing buildings, AHMM was in tune with a new vision of Broadgate. Michael Meadows, the company's Head of Planning, stresses the sustainable credentials of the project: 'the flexibility and adaptability of the original designs has enabled us to reimagine the building for the future', he says. British Land's Head of Office Leasing, Michael Wiseman, places AHMM's project in the context of the original Arup scheme, which responded to the emergence of the City as the pre-eminent global financial centre. 'Now, 30 years later, AHMM have re-imagined this 80s classic to meet the needs of another industry experiencing significant growth, as London's tech scene flourishes and this area establishes itself as Europe's answer to Silicon Valley', Wiseman says. 'The combination of classic architecture, large, efficient floorplates and a radical reworking of the interior have struck a chord with the new wave of pioneering businesses who see the building as the ideal platform to continue their growth in London'. The essential elements that made the building remarkable have been retained and skillfully exploited. In many respects, Peter Foggo's vision of the early 1980s has only been brought fully to fruition in a new century and in a City of London transformed in the last quarter of a century.

FIG.54:
Following spread: Upper Atrium gantry, viewed from Level 3.

1 FA

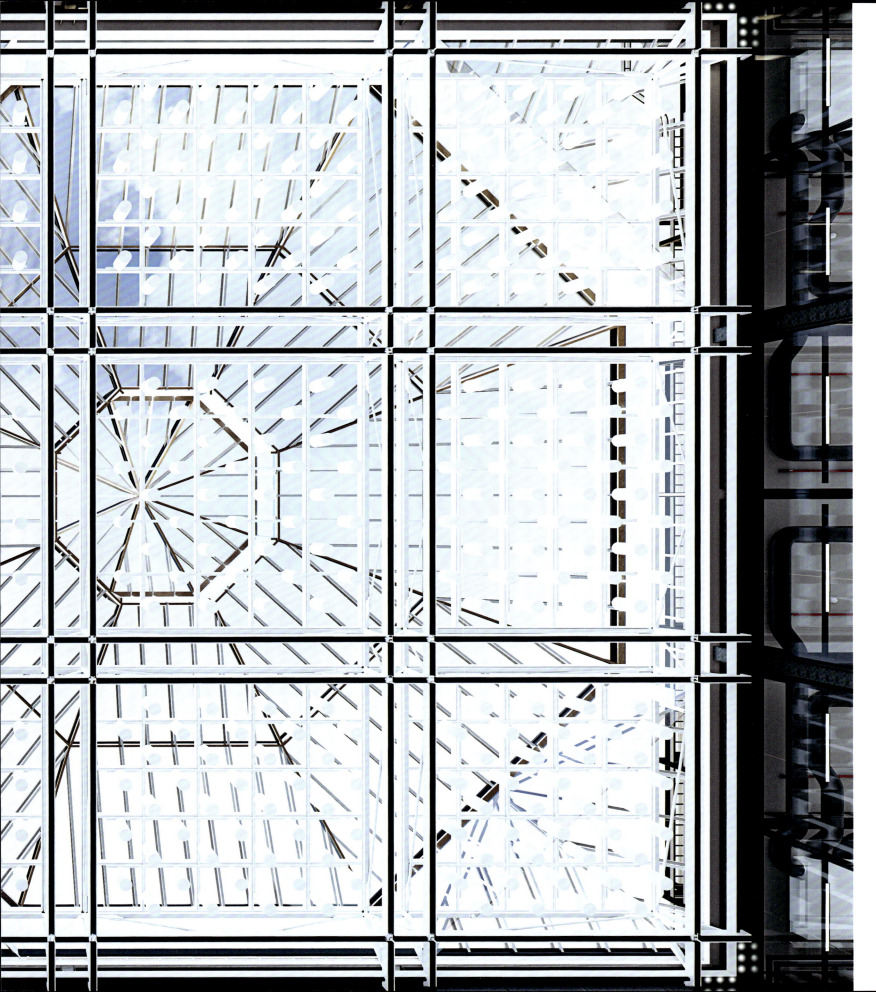

Building 1 Finsbury Avenue

THE BUILDING IN USE

THE BUILDING IN USE

In June 1984, Rosehaugh Greycoat was able to announce that more than half the space at 1 Finsbury Avenue, a total of 126,500 sq.ft (11,750 sq.m), had been let before the completion of the building. Stockbrokers Rowe & Pitman had exchanged contracts on the sixth and seventh floors, stockbrokers L. Messel & Co. had taken the third floor and solicitors Barlow, Lyde & Gilbert the second floor. Tenants had been attracted, it was stated, by 'the large floors, flexible services, low energy costs and the dramatic visual impact of the building'. The remainder of the building would soon be let at a rent of £19.75 per square foot, with the landlord contributing £5 per square foot to cover fitting-out costs. The critical reception of the building was extremely positive. The *Architectural Review* commented that 'Arups have provided an object lesson for all architects. They prove that spec offices can make a sensitive contribution to a civic environment, and that even a huge office building can have a richness and delicate scale suggestive of the human beings who work within'.[1] The architectural critics focused on the exterior of the building and its urban presence. Internally, it was subdivided as largely cellular office space, with the open atrium the focus of the building – its ground floor a space open to the public. The benefits offered by 1 Finsbury Avenue, a marketing brochure stated, were radically novel. (fig.37)

From multiple to single tenants

The multi-tenanted occupation of the building worked well – a reflection of its adaptable design. This was 'a truly cost-effective office'. The letting agents proclaimed it as a 'new generation office complex', offering 'three large advantages which add up to one enormous cost benefit'. Firstly, the building was remarkably flexible; its large floors offered freedom of layout, with minimal constraints on partitioning – 'every square foot of space is usable'. Secondly, it was designed for low-energy operation: 'Finsbury Avenue will need half as much energy as most other buildings in the City of London'. Finally, 'the shell and core system makes it possible to fit out the offices without the waste of a single penny'. Tenants could either take the standard fit-out – raised floors, suspended ceilings, light fittings and wall coverings – or start with the bare shell and core, with the building left as a structural shell, and specify their own fit-out. The building was highly energy-efficient thanks to the use of external shading, double glazing and insulation. 'The techniques of heating and cooling are highly efficient. Flexible ducts direct air conditioning where it is needed, and the curtain walls diffuse comfortable radiant heat'. In terms of office layout, the building offered various options: 'at least 85% of the space spans 45 feet [13.7m] from window to atrium window: this is a particularly happy module because it makes any office layout possible – from totally cellular to totally open plan, or any combination. This total flexibility enables tenants to grow in number without spreading in space'. Raised floors containing cables for power, phones and data communication were another key element in the building's agenda of flexibility. Cables could be quickly and inexpensively rerouted. The building was, however, 'much more than just an exercise in technology. For here technology has taken interesting shape: no two floors are the same, perspectives catch you with surprises, there are trees and water and varieties of texture and moments of visual drama. Technology can live happily enough in boxes, but human beings need buildings'.

The acquisition of Rowe & Pitman and another City firm – Mullens, Akroyd and Smithers – by S.G. Warburg in 1986 led to the last-named company's expansion: it became the sole occupant of 1 Finsbury Avenue. The building, judged 'retrofit friendly', was adapted to house 500 dealers in readiness for the 'Big Bang'.[2] In 1991, British Land acquired 1, 2 and 3 Finsbury Avenue, a

FIG.55
Level 3 office
before refurbishment.

FIG.56
Lower Atrium
before refurbishment.

FIG.57:
The Upper Atrium, before refurbishment.

The Building in Use

FIG.58:
The Upper Atrium, after refurbishment.

FIGS 59 & 60:
Office floor showing the integration of the structure and exposed services.

prelude to its acquisition of the entire Broadgate Estate five years later. By 1995, S.G. Warburg had merged with the Swiss Bank Corporation to form SBC Warburg, latterly Warburg Dillon Read. The new entity – later merged into UBS – required a base for its dealer operations. It vacated offices in Lower Thames Street in order to focus its operations at Finsbury Avenue, where it planned to house 1200 dealers in radically upgraded surroundings. Arup Associates, led by Mick Brundle, was appointed by British Land to review the options for adapting the existing building, which had been designed to be multi-tenanted. 'The vision of the designers was to create a major market place in the heart of 1 Finsbury Avenue in which every dealer would feel involved in the excitement and energy generated on the dealer floor'.[3] To create the necessary space for dealers, it was proposed to floor over the atrium at third-floor level – rather than at second floor, as first suggested – creating

a large new dealing floor linked by new stairs to the fourth and fifth floors. This was potentially controversial since 1 Finsbury Avenue was already recognised as an outstanding building of its period. The Twentieth Century Society questioned the need for radical change, but, after extended discussion, resolved not to object. Clearly, Number 1 was an exceptional building of its period – but was little more than a decade old. English Heritage had, at this time, not yet listed any building of such recent vintage and only two buildings dating from the 1970s were listed. When the DOCOMOMO group submitted a formal request for the building to be listed, EH made a visit and discussed the proposals with the architects and owners. The visiting party 'considered the proposals to be well designed and architecturally exciting'. It was clear, they added, that 'Foggo did not intend that the office interiors should be judged in any assessment of the building'. Some of those inspected 'were in a poor

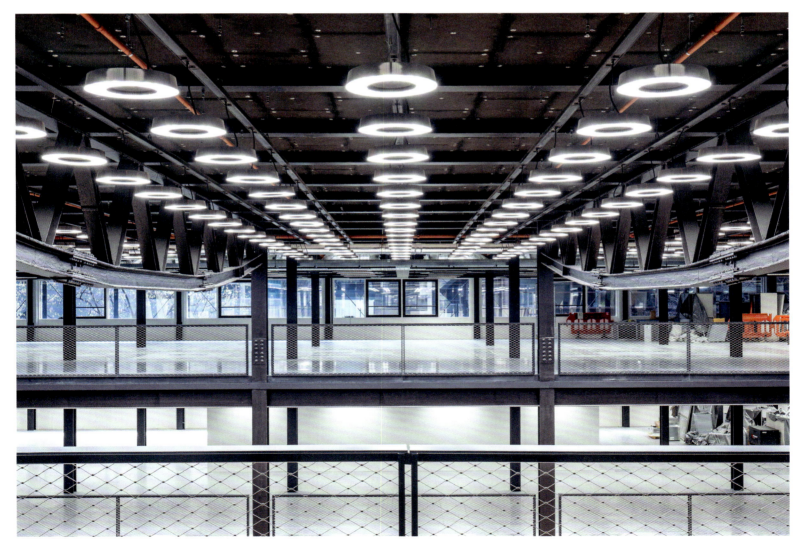

"designers" Victorian style'.[4] The conclusion was that the building lacked the special interest necessary for a listing at Grade II* – necessary for any building less than 30 years old. English Heritage somewhat regretted the necessity for altering the building, but accepted the rationale for change. The listing request was rejected.

The Arup scheme went on site in August 1996, and dealers were able to move into the new floor a year later – with final completion of the scheme in July 1998. Services were significantly upgraded, with much-enhanced cooling, using an underfloor supply system with the floor void as a supply-air plenum and the ceiling void for return air. The now enclosed ground-floor lobby was relit. Thus upgraded, the building worked well for the best part of two decades, intensively occupied by UBS.

Listing – and an Arup redesign

The issue of listing resurfaced in the face of UBS' impending vacation of the building. A recommendation that the Arup blocks forming the first phase of Broadgate (fig.62) should be listed was made by English Heritage. Even admirers of Peter Foggo's work had their doubts about the move. Rab Bennetts, who had been part of the team that designed 1 Finsbury Avenue, commented that 'everything about Broadgate seemed too fast for its own good'.[5] Yet Broadgate was a hugely successful mix of public space and commercial buildings that became a landmark in British development history. English Heritage, opposed to the demolition of 4 and 6 Broadgate to make way for the new UBS London headquarters designed by architects MAKE, submitted its recommendation to then Culture Secretary Jeremy Hunt. It was a daring proposal: the buildings put forward for listing were little more than two decades old and constituted a virtual City district. Listing the Arup buildings would derail British Land's plans for MAKE's new 700,000 sq.ft (65,000 sq.m) UBS building on the site of 4 and 6 Broadgate and housing 6000 staff (the scheme had already gained planning consent from the City). The City of London Corporation made its views clear: it regarded the prospect of Broadgate being listed, and UBS quitting the City, as disastrous. 'The City is, and always has been, first and foremost, a place of business and it must be allowed to meet the long-term business needs of current and potential future occupiers'. In June 2011, Jeremy Hunt announced that the listing submission had been rejected. A certificate of immunity from listing was issued in respect of Numbers 4 and 6, allowing UBS' scheme for the site to proceed. In 2013, Hunt's successor as Culture Secretary, Maria Miller, authorised the issue of a certificate of immunity for the remaining Arup buildings at Broadgate, opening the way for the redevelopment of the campus. A move by the Twentieth Century Society to have 1 and 2 Broadgate listed – in the face of a redevelopment scheme by architects AHMM – was unsuccessful. With the backing of what was by now Historic England, a certificate of immunity from listing was issued in 2018 and the way was open for redevelopment. (A similar certificate in respect of 2 and 3 Finsbury Avenue was issued in 2015, and has since been renewed.)

The Arup blocks on Finsbury Avenue were not included in the 2011 listing submission. In spring 2013, the Twentieth Century Society submitted an application for the listing of Number 1. This came in the context of an ongoing research project by English Heritage (soon to be reborn as Historic England) to assess commercial buildings dating from the mid-1960s to the mid-1980s for potential listing. In the aftermath of the rejection of the earlier Broadgate listing submission, the project involved consultation with building owners. British Land, conscious of the special interest of Number 1 but concerned about its future commercial viability, engaged in a fruitful dialogue with Historic England. The way in

FIG.61
New restaurants lead on to Finsbury Avenue Square.

FIG.62:
Broadgate Circle.

which the building had been altered since its completion, notably the infilling of the atrium, was noted. The recent relocation of UBS to 5 Broadgate meant that the building had to find a new role in a changing City and Historic England responded to this issue, conceding the potential for change. The possible addition of two new floors was one major alteration to the building that was taken on board (though subsequently not progressed). The Grade II listing of Number 1 was announced in January 2015 – it was one of four Arup Associates projects included in a total of 14 buildings listed, a recognition of the pre-eminent role of the practice in progressive office design over several decades. British Land expressed its satisfaction that the listing was in tune with its vision for the future development of Broadgate 'as an exemplar of flexible and adaptable commercial place-making'. The retention of the public spaces that were key to the whole concept of the development was an essential element in the company's vision for Broadgate. As Nigel Webb, British Land's long-standing Head of Developments, has pointed out, the City and neighbouring quarters of Tower Hamlets and Hackney have undergone radical change since the 1980s. British Land's vision is, he says, of 'a world class, seven day a week, mixed use central London destination' – a vision that appears to resonate with the occupants of the area, and which is strongly endorsed by the City planners.

Historic England's listing description of 1 Finsbury Avenue notes that the building's special interest 'resides particularly in the external envelope, where the form, structure and aesthetic are unaltered'. It was 'a rigorously designed "shell and core" building, designed to be fully flexible internally'. The description further notes the changes made to the building in 1997, and states that 'all structural intervention and changes to the fabric made in 1997 and thereafter are excluded from the

FIG.63:
Finsbury Avenue Square.

listing'. Basement levels and the interiors of ground-floor commercial units were also excluded. The listing was the outcome of extended discussions with British Land, and provided the basis for a sensitive programme of changes to the building in order to ensure its future.

A change of architect

The listing of 1 Finsbury Avenue was followed by a process of negotiation with Historic England – the building had to be re-equipped for the future. Initially, Arup Associates was appointed to progress a refurbishment project for the building – including a two-storey rooftop extension, which won planning and listed building consent in autumn 2015. (fig.40) However, in autumn 2016, British Land and its partner GIC appointed AHMM to progress the project. The brief from British Land was to work in tune with the existing fabric – opening up the ground floor and reinstating the public route through the building, connecting it to the wider area of Broadgate. British Land's vision for the building was clear. As Nigel Webb comments, 'the iconic nature of the architecture lends itself to a broad range of users and new entrants to the City. Far from appearing dated, the building has the feel of a modern classic'. David Lockyer, Head of Broadgate, insists, 'we have retained the original character of the building externally but reimagined it internally – by exposing services, creating dramatic and characterful spaces and providing access to external terraces. This has played a huge part in attracting a new type of occupier to Broadgate and the City'. For Lockyer, the project epitomises the changing character of Broadgate – 'more active and connected, with retail, restaurant and leisure uses…'.[6]

Emily Gee, Historic England's Regional Director of Planning for London and the South East, recalls the process of negotiation: 'we recognised that the building no longer met the needs of the changing City of London.

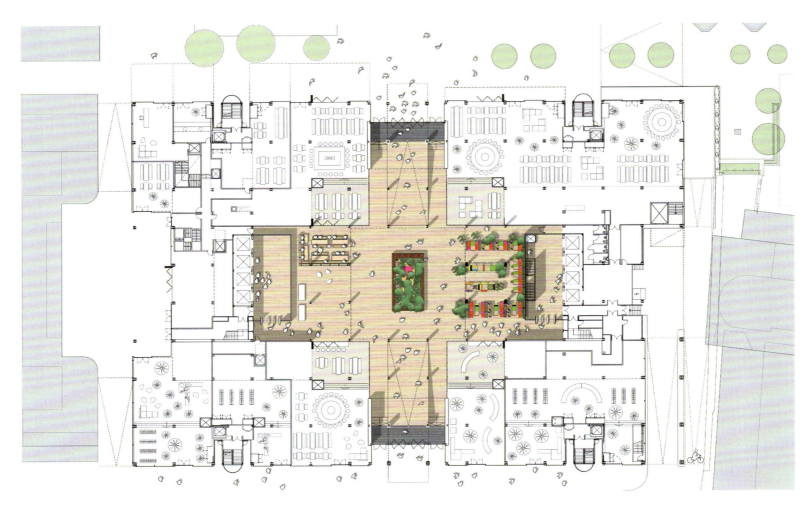

FIG.64:
AHMM ground floor plan.

British Land saw its potential – there was the basis for fruitful collaboration based on an understanding of the building. A project emerged that was about allowing the architecture to talk'.[7] Gee's colleague at Historic England, Michael Dunn, adds that 'it helped that British Land appreciated the quality of the building – it wasn't hard to come to an agreement on its future'.[8] In June 2017, consent for a programme of refurbishment, designed by AHMM to give 1 Finsbury Avenue a viable future, was granted.

Michael Meadows, British Land's Head of Planning, comments, 'we worked closely with Historic England and the City of London to agree the listing description and potential for change to the building. This was critical to the success of the project – a matter of preserving and enhancing the building's character and heritage, but recognizing the potential to reimagine it for the 21st century'.[9] Nigel Webb adds, 'we were happy to work with Historic England to agree, in effect, a consensual listing in 2015 which allowed for the refurbishment and repositioning of the building to meet modern workplace standards while respecting, and even enhancing, its special interest'.[10] In many respects, indeed, the renaissance of 1 Finsbury Avenue is a pioneering example of collaboration – it provides a marker for a future dialogue between the property industry and the guardians of our heritage.

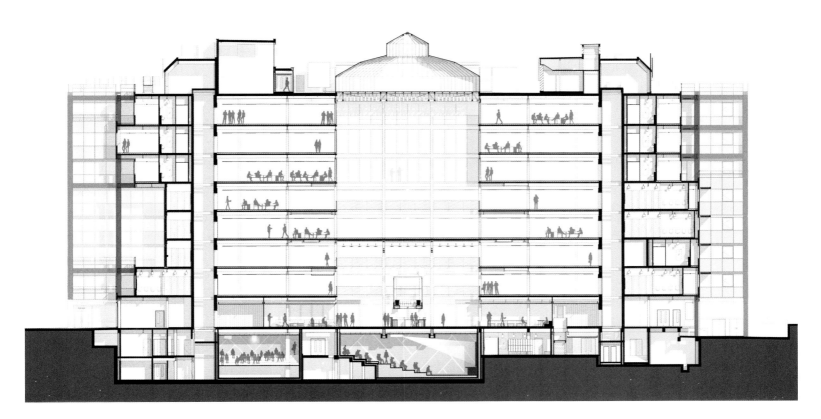

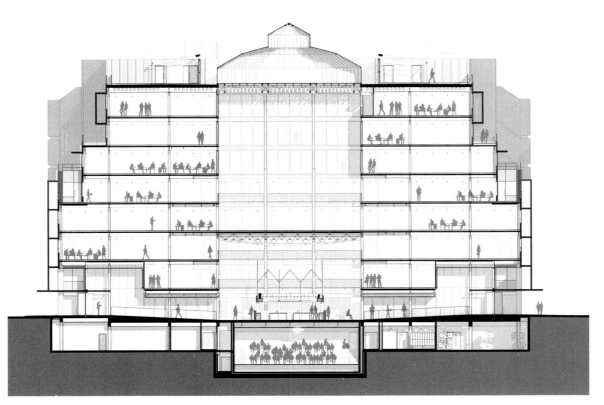

FIGS 65 & 66:
AHMM drawings showing long and cross sections of the building.

The Building in Use

EQUIPPING THE BUILDING FOR THE FUTURE

EQUIPPING THE BUILDING FOR THE FUTURE

The listing of 1 Finsbury Avenue in January 2015 was the outcome of extended negotiations between English Heritage – to become Historic England a few months later – and British Land. The provision in the listing that the special interest of the building 'resides particularly in the external envelope, where the form, structure and aesthetic are unaltered' was highly significant. Indeed, it reflected Frank Duffy's concept of 'shell, services, scenery and sets'. Peter Foggo had insisted that 'the design must recognize the difference between those parts of the building with a long stable life span and those where constant change, wide variation in aesthetic character and short life are principal characteristics'.[1] The listing, reflecting this strategy, excluded 'all internal fixtures and fittings', along with the basement levels and ground-floor commercial units. The building's adaptability was noted as part of its special interest.

AHMM

Appointed by British Land, in February 2017, to develop a scheme for the refurbishment of the listed building, Allford Hall Monaghan Morris, led by partner Paul Monaghan, working with structural and services engineers at Arup, led by Michael Beaven, developed a project to give 1 Finsbury Avenue a profitable future in the context of a rapidly changing City scene. The basic aim of the project, as launched by British Land, was 'to retain/reuse/recondition'. The objective was to address the needs of potential users very different from the bankers who had previously occupied the building. The likely tenants would be drawn from the new-tech/creative-industries sector, which had colonised the area around Old Street, on the City fringe, north of Broadgate.

AHMM was established in 1989 by Simon Allford, Jonathan Hall, Paul Monaghan and Peter Morris, and is now a major presence on the British architectural scene.

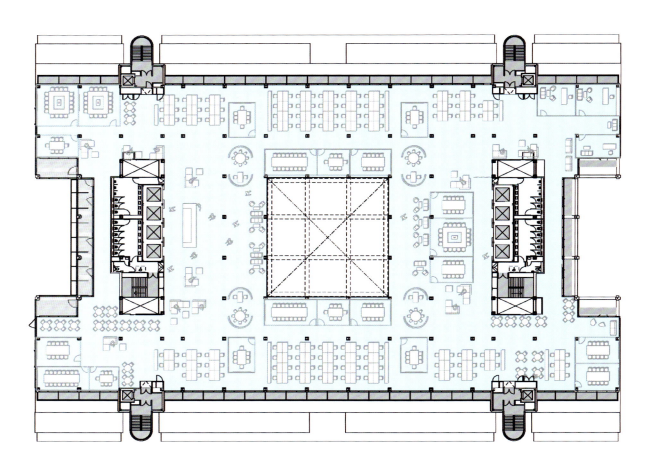

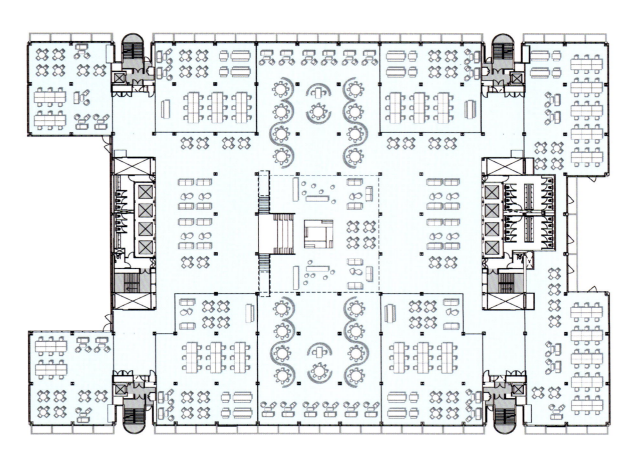

FIGS 67–69:
AHMM plans of the built refurbishment showing Levels 3 (far left, below), 5 (left) and 8 (below).

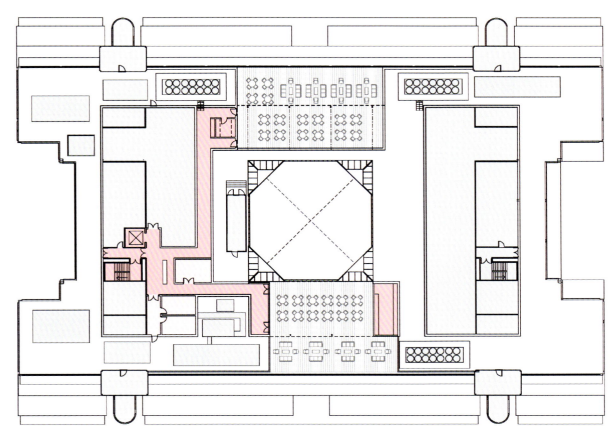

FIGS 70:
Left: Original concept ground floor plan.

FIG.71:
Right: West façade from Wilson Street.

FIG.72:
Following spread: Storey flexible workspace on Level 2.

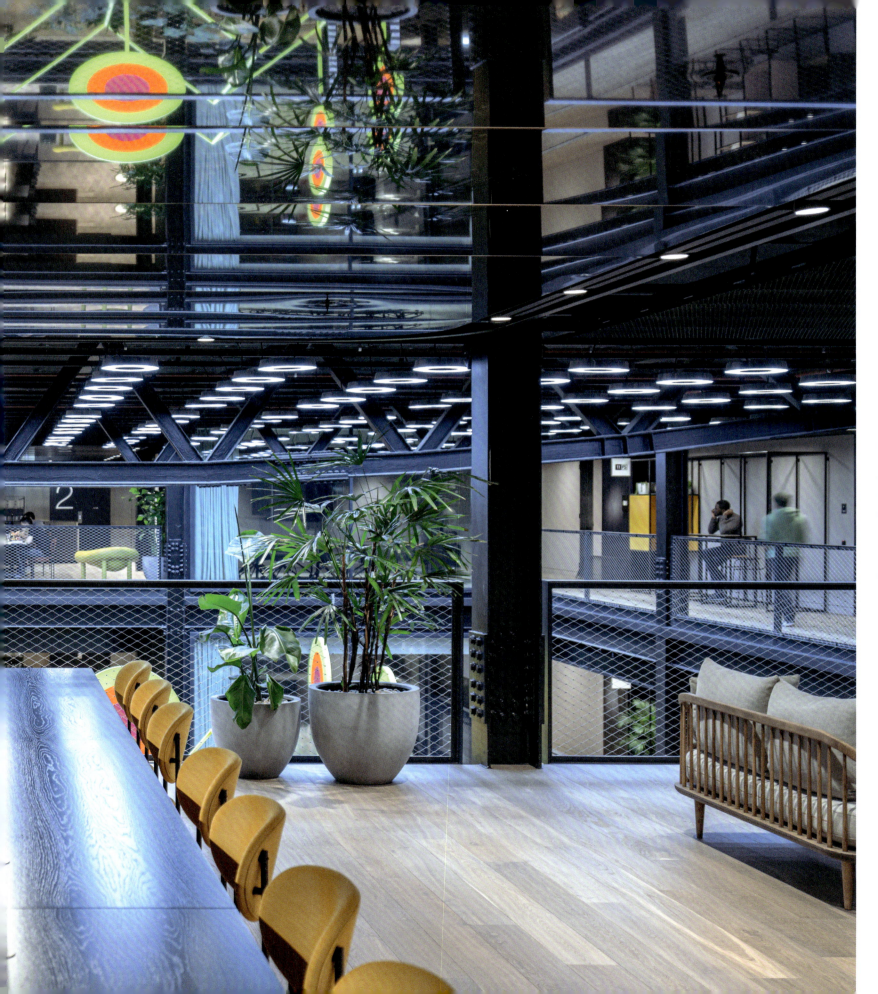

Equipping the Building for the Future

FIG:73:
Washrooms in art deco colours.

FIG.74:
The roof terrace.

The refurbishment and reimagining of existing buildings is a significant element in the practice's workload. The mixed-use redevelopment of the former BBC Television Centre in west London, the conversion of a 1930s' block on the Thames Embankment to house New Scotland Yard, the refashioning of the Barbican Arts Centre and the 'reinvention' of Liverpool's Royal Court Theatre are projects that exemplify its approach. The practice is also responsible for the redevelopment of 1 and 2 Broadgate, given planning consent in early 2019.

AHMM's appointment for the 1 Finsbury Avenue project in 2017 led to a reassessment of the Arup Associates scheme, which had been consented in 2015. This had provided, most significantly, for the addition of two new floors, making a major impact on the building. The ground floor of the building was left relatively unchanged. The client brief to AHMM demanded a more radical approach, creating an enhanced connection to the Broadgate estate and a more welcoming strategy for the streetscape, emphasising the permeability of the building. British Land's aim was to 'position the building as a next generation hub for tech and creative businesses and a catalyst for change at Broadgate': in line with a policy of diversifying the Broadgate campus to attract a wider range of occupiers, 'we want to open up the ground and experiment with uses which draw people to 1 FA to create an integrated mixed-use building'. AHMM's response to this challenging brief was radical. It envisaged the transformation of a corporate office building into one with a mix of uses, with 'work, rest and play' provided for. The ground floor would be made welcoming and permeable as part of a 'reboot' of the building, 'a complete transformation and reimaging of the building to attract a new demographic: the tech-creative occupier'. As part of this process of re-imaging, the building should be stripped back to its basic structure – the project should embrace 'an honesty in the exposing

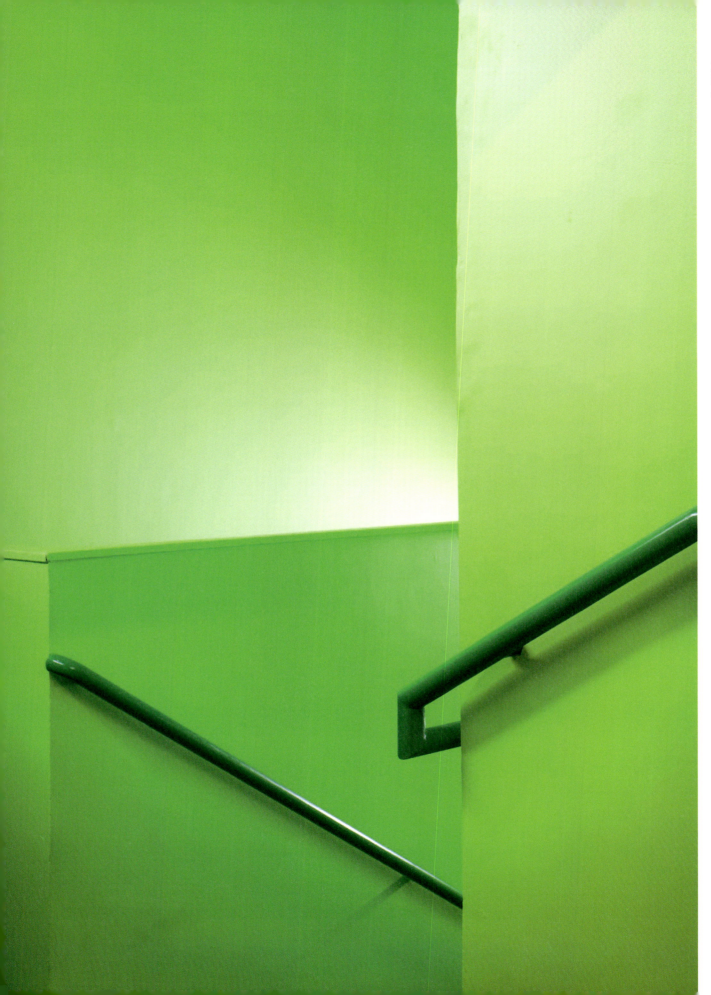

FIG:75:
Each staircase has its own vibrant colour scheme.

FIG.76:
Following spread: Atoll seating area in Ground Floor reception.

Equipping the Building for the Future

FIG.77:
A ground floor retail area opens into the Lower Atrium.

FIGS 78 & 79:
Whitecross Place before and after the bridges and canopy were removed.

of the existing structure and what materials are put back in'. The key to AHMM's design was 'embracing the as found'.

The transformation of 1 Finsbury Avenue

One important aspect of AHMM's approach to 1 Finsbury Avenue was the reinstatement of public access at ground-floor level, with the through pedestrian route from Wilson Street to Finsbury Avenue Square reopened and the ground floor of the building turned into a lively public space, with cafés and restaurants extending into the square. The ground floor was to be reinstated as the heart of the building, open to all. The option of reinstating the full-height atrium, with the 1990s' infill removed, having been rejected, the upper atrium became the focus of the office floors.

A major feature of AHMM's approach is the stripping back of the interior, with the encasements on the columns removed (in favour of a layer of black intumescent paint) and ceiling panelling, concealing services, equally dispensed with. The building is taken back to its bare bones – the results, a raw aesthetic, might not be in tune with bankers' taste but reflect the ethos of a very different set of users and the architects' objective of 'a complete transformation and re-imaging' of the building to address their needs. Nothing is concealed.

In the context of the building's Grade II listing, which stated that its special interest lay chiefly in its exterior, the treatment of the external envelope was obviously a critical aspect of AHMM's scheme. With restaurant and retail use proposed at ground level, the heavy granite cladding to piers and spandrels was removed to maximise the usable frontage. Along with the granite plinths, existing stairs and smoke vents were also removed to allow the existing street surface to meet the

FIG:80:
Left: Interior communal spaces in 1 Finsbury Avenue.

FIG:81:
Right: Artwork by Studio Myerscough.

FIG. 82:
Following spread: Artwork by Studio Myserscough

1 FA

FIG.83:
Everyman Cinema corridor.

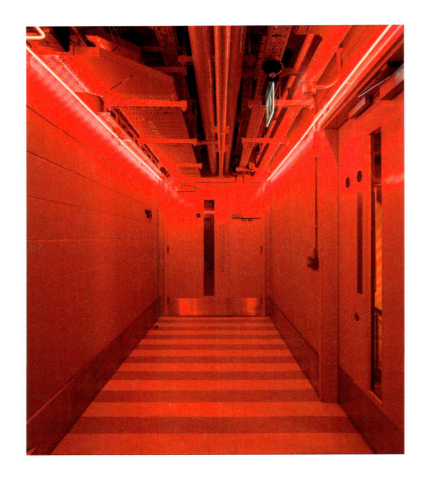

glazing line. Working with Arup Facades, the architects were able to specify cladding for the ground floor of the building to closely match the existing one. The impact of the changes was to open up the building in a way that might not have been appropriate for its previous occupants. The transformation is equally apparent in the treatment of the ground floor, with its range of eating places, and in the colonisation of the roof – previously the domain of plant rooms, generators and other equipment – as another amenity for those working in the building. At every level, the building has been opened up by creating access to the existing external terraces, originally used only for maintenance, to form break-out spaces to the offices. The Everyman cinema with three screens, occupying 11,000 sq.ft (1000 sq.m) of space at ground-floor and basement level on the north-east corner of the building, is another radically new facility for the Broadgate estate. (An entire floor was removed from the basement level to create the necessary space.)

It reflects British Land's progressive vision of 1 Finsbury Avenue as a seven-day-a-week building, not one that is largely empty from Friday evening until Monday morning.

AHMM's transformation of 1 Finsbury Avenue is dramatic – yet, in many respects, conservative in that it reflects the original aspirations of Peter Foggo and his team. Ideas of completely replacing the façade were rejected: in Michael Beaven of Arup's view, this would have been a wasteful extravagance. Indeed, Arup's analysis of the building generated what is, perhaps surprisingly, a highly conservative restoration that respected the quality of what existed. Reusing and reinventing the existing building, minimising waste and recycling materials were fundamental ingredients of the project. The emphasis was on adapting and reusing as much of what existed as possible – services as well as the basic structure. The project was both environmentally friendly and, equally, tailored to the needs of a new

FIGS 84–85:
Everyman Cinema, Screen 1.

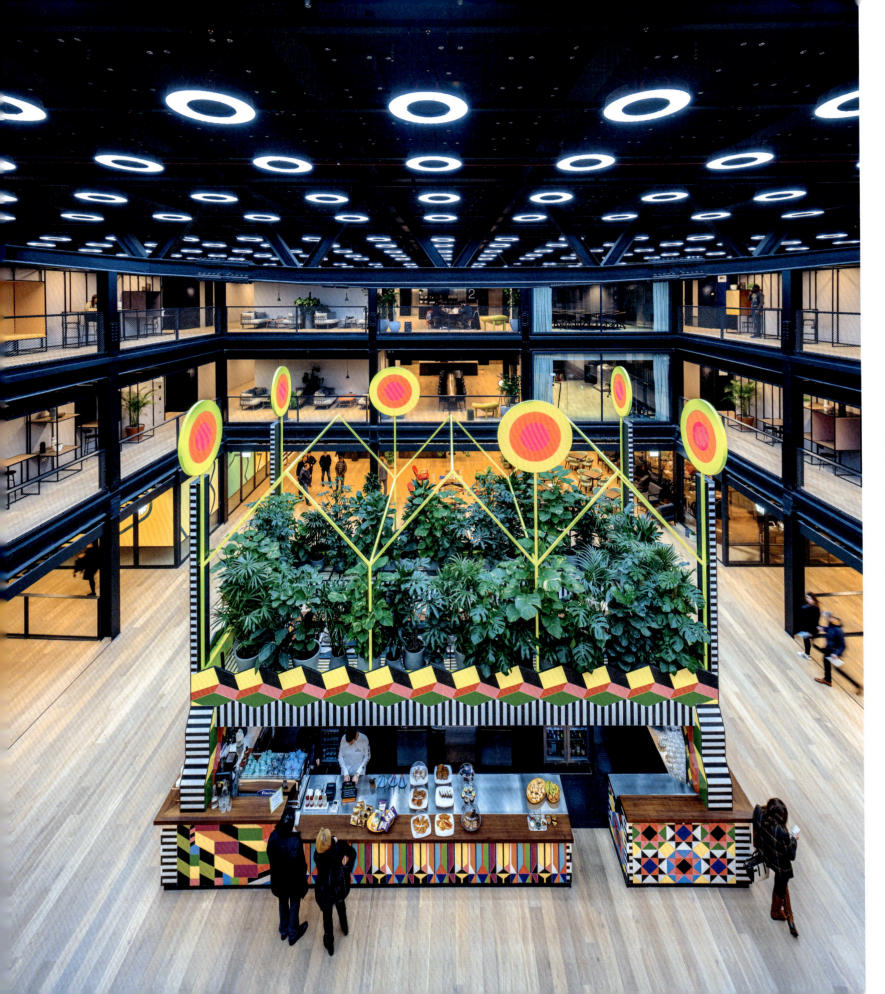

Equipping the Building for the Future

1 FA

generation of users. The servicing strategy for the original building had been highly innovative in its time, but was significantly modified as part of the mid-1990s' refit carried out by Arup Associates. The façade of the building was a key element in the 2015 listing, 'flowing around the whole building like a giant external radiator', as Beaven describes it. On examination, it was found to be remarkably close to modern standards in terms of insulation, solar gain and airtightness – modest upgrading was all that was required. As part of the refurbishment project, 'top down' cooling, with fan-coil systems using chilled water, was reinstated in place of the underfloor system installed in the 1990s (and necessitated by the very heavy cooling load imposed by the arrival of 1200 dealers). The installation of a digital Smart system allows building managers to control the heating and cooling of the building.[2] As a consequence of the rethink of services, the roof of the building was freed of much of the clutter it had acquired since the 1980s. The exposure of the previously concealed services internally, with the removal of ceiling panels, was part of a process of rediscovering the building, giving it a dramatically functional look that would surely win the approval of Peter Foggo. A particular challenge was posed by the transformation of the ground floor to house restaurants and cafés – greatly enhanced services were required in addition to the requirements of the basement cinema. The aesthetic of 1 Finsbury Avenue as refurbished by AHMM – stripped back to its bare bones, the austere dignity of Foggo's architecture revealed – is in tune with a new breed of user. This is a building that is now historic, but is re-equipped for a dynamic future in the London of the twenty-first century.

Nigel Webb of British Land sums up what has been achieved in the reinvention of 1 Finsbury Avenue:

> we are delighted with the end result and the quality of space that it provides. The building has been re-energised while retaining its iconic design. New roof terraces, the introduction of retail and leisure uses and active ground floor frontages work with the grain of the original architecture while adding a new dynamism to the building and the spaces around it, making it more permeable and open to the City. AHMM's successful redesign of the building has been reflected in our leasing success, with all the space let before practical completion.[3]

The reinvention of 1 Finsbury Avenue, as one element in British Land's renewal of Broadgate, is the outcome of a dialogue between two sectors – property and heritage – that are too often seen as at odds. The building has proved an ideal base for the new industries that are breathing fresh life into the City. It is a heritage asset, but also a dynamic agent of change and renewal.

FIG.88:
Rush Hour sculpture by George Segal at the entrance to 1 Finsbury Avenue

Afterword
PAUL MONAGHAN

Director, Allford Hall Monaghan Morris
August 2019

I first became aware of 1FA in my final year at the Bartlett. It was the first 'spec' office building to be featured in the *Architectural Review* and it was designed by a prestigious practice, Arup Associates, a firm the four of us admired hugely. Up until that point, with a few exceptions, only commercial practices designed offices and the design quality was never that high.

Our (AHMM) final joint diploma project, 'The Fifth Man', focused on the new emerging Big Bang offices with their huge floor plates to house dealing rooms. We were excited by this new typology and wrote to Peter Foggo to see if we could meet him to discuss 1FA and his emerging designs for Broadgate. His PA told us he was too busy, but a few days later Peter rang us and invited us over to his office one evening. He was designing the new buildings around the Circus (Broadgate Circle) and was complaining how quickly the designs had to be completed. He didn't know what the Circus was going to be but suggested that it could be an ice rink, which seemed quite odd at the time.

He talked through the steel and composite-floor techniques used on 1FA that Stuart Lipton had brought over from the US, and how it provided fast-track construction. It was clear Stuart was very involved with the design process – even ringing Peter on Sunday mornings with new ideas!

It's been a privilege working on the rebooting of this building. Our practice believes that well-designed buildings can live through multiple reinventions, and the robust nature of 1FA makes this easy. We've been very careful with any new interventions to make sure they complement the existing building. Once we stripped the internal finishes of the building and exposed the fine detailing of the structure, we decided our new elements such as balustrades and ceilings would be more industrial in their character.

As an accent, we brought in Studio Myerscough to design the café and wall paintings that form an important centrepiece at the entrance and announce the reimagining of what will become a more public building.

I wish I could have met with Peter Foggo again to see if he approved. I think he would have enjoyed the idea of removing all those bland suspended ceilings and the idea of making the ground floor more active with restaurants and a cinema. In some ways all we've done is uncovered the beauty and integrity of his original building.

NOTES

Prelude: BEFORE THE RAILWAYS
1. *Architectural Review*, 177, 1059, May 1985, p.23.
2. Robert Thorne, *Liverpool Street Station* (London, Academy Editions, 1978), p.27.

THE COMING OF THE RAILWAYS
1. John Betjeman, *London's Historic Railway Stations* (London, John Murray, 1972), p.50.
2. Alan A. Jackson, *London's Termini* (Newton Abbot, David & Charles, 1969), p.108.
3. Betjeman, op.cit., p.50; Jackson, op.cit., p.96.
4. ibid, p.50.
5. *Great Eastern Magazine,* February 1923, p.23. For a detailed history of the station, see Robert Thorne, *Liverpool Street Station* (London, Academy Editions, 1978).
6. Betjeman, op.cit., pp 30, 35.
7. Ian Nairn, *Nairn's London* (Harmondsworth, Penguin, 1966), p.42.
8. Tom Driberg quoted in Thorne, op.cit., p.63.

PLANNING BATTLES
1. Alan A. Jackson, *London's Termini* (Newton Abbot, David & Charles, 1969), p.54. In 2019, 1970s' office buildings subsequently developed adjacent to the station were being demolished for the HS2 project.
2. See Kenneth Powell, *St Pancras, London* (London, Manhattan Loft Corporation, 2011), pp 60–4; Simon Bradley, *St Pancras Station* (London, Profile Books, 2007), pp 157–60.
3. Inspector's Report from public inquiry, August 1977 – LMA, GLC/TD/TP/FT/07/007 (1), p.11.
4. ibid., p.10.
5. See Nick Derbyshire, *Liverpool Street: A station for the twenty-first century* (Cambridge, Granta Editions, 1991), pp 48–75.
6. See letter of 5 March 1985, from EH Chief Executive Peter Rumble to the Department of the Environment – LMA/GLC/AR/HB/02/3591.

CLIENT AND ARCHITECT
1. See Penelope Hunting, *Cutlers Gardens* (London, Standard Life Assurance Company, 1984).
2. See Kenneth Powell, *Arup Associates* (London, Historic England, 2018).
3. ibid., p.12.
4. ibid., p.17. The Horizon Factory was under demolition in 2019, following the failure of a campaign for its listing. See also John Carter, "Management contracting: the Horizon project", *Architects' Journal*, 14 February, 1973, pp 395–400.
5. *Architects' Journal*, 2 August 1983, p.34.
6. Stuart Lipton, in conversation with the author, 25 January 2019.
7. ibid.
8. Letter in Arup archives.
9. 'Something in the City', *Building Design*, 12 August 1994, p.12.

DESIGNING 1 FINSBURY AVENUE
1. Stuart Lipton, in conversation with the author, 25 January 2019.
2. *Architects' Journal*, 27 February 1985, pp 30–2.
3. Rab Bennetts, 'A personal perspective', unpublished paper, 2011.
4. Ian Taylor, in conversation with the author, 21 January 2019.
5. Bennetts, op.cit.
6. *Building Design*, 12 August 1994, p.12.
7. John Ritblat, in conversation with the author, 26 March 2019. See John Weston Smith, *No Stone Upturned: A History of the British Land Company 1856-2006* (London, British Land, 2006), p.61.
8. Stuart Lipton, in conversation with the author, 25 January 2019.
9. Unpublished paper, '1 Finsbury Avenue: 1979-83, and thereafter', 2019.
10. ibid.

BUILDING 1 FINSBURY AVENUE
1. Paul Lewis in discussion with the author, 13 March 2019.
2. *Architects' Journal*, 24/31 August 1983, p.66.
3. ibid., p.67.
4. ibid.
5. *Designers' Journal*, January 1985, p.38.
6. Tony Taylor, 'Current developments in structural steel', lecture delivered at Reading University, 24 March 1988.
7. Simon Bradley and Nikolaus Pevsner, *The Buildings of England, London 1: The City of London* (London, Penguin, 1997), p.436.
8. Stuart Lipton, interview with the author, 25 January 2019.
9. Letter to Foggo, dated 23 November 1982: Arup archives.

10 *Architects' Journal*, 21/28 December 1988, p.49.
11 *Architectural Review*, 177, 1059, May 1985, p.30.
12 ibid.
13 *Architects' Journal*, 25 September 1985, p.28.
14 Tony Taylor, in conversation with the author, 25 January 2019; 'Statement on the significance and architectural details of 1 Finsbury Avenue', dated 30 May 2014.
15 Letter in Arup archives, dated 7 December 1982.
16 Colin Davies, 'Best laid plans', *Designers' Journal*, January 1985, p.30.
17 ibid., p.37.
18 Hugh Pearman, 'Developing ideas', *Designers' Journal*, January 1985, p.38.
19 ibid., p.38.
20 Chris Strickland, in conversation with the author, 7 March 2019.
21 Nigel Webb, in conversation with the author, 11 June 2019.

THE BUILDING IN USE

1 Peter Buchanan, 'Urban Arups', *Architectural Review*, 177, 1059, May 1985, p.30.
2 See Graham Ridout, 'Good connections', *Building*, 16 May 1986, pp 46–8.
3 *Arup Journal*, 35/1, 2000, p.15.
4 English Heritage agenda for committee meetings, March 1996.
5 Rab Bennetts, 'Separating fact from fiction on Broadgate', unpublished paper, 2011.
6 David Lockyer, in conversation with the author.
7 Emily Gee, in conversation with the author, 1 April 2019.
8 Michael Dunn, in conversation with the author, 1 April 2019.
9 Michael Meadows, emailed quotes from British Land.
10 Nigel Webb, in conversation with the author.

EQUIPPING THE BUILDING FOR THE FUTURE

1 *Designers' Journal*, January 1985, p.29.
2 See *Arup Journal*, 35/1, 2000, pp 17–18.
3 Nigel Webb, in conversation with the author.

INDEX

Numbers refer to page numbers; numbers in *italics* indicate illustrations.

Allford Hall Monaghan Morris (AHMM) 40, 77, 100, 106, 111, 116, 121
Andaz Liverpool Street Hotel 15
Arup Associates 37, 43, 46, 56, 57, 59, 60, 63, 67, 77, 79, 84, 90, 93, 94, 95, 116, 121
Ashbee, W.N. 25

Baker, William 18
Barry Jnr, Charles 22
Barry, Sir Charles 22
Beaven, Michael 100, 116, 121
Bennetts, Rab 52, 59
Betjeman, Sir John 18, 20, 25, 28, 31
Bovis Ltd 46
Bradman, Godfrey 34, 59, 63
British Land 40, 59, 84, 90, 94, 95, 96, 100, 106, 121
British Transport Commission 28
Broad Street Station 18, *19*, 20, *22*, 28, 31, 32, *36*, 37
Broadgate Circle *94*
Brown, George 28
Buchanan, Peter 14, 77

Casson, Sir Hugh 32
Crystal Palace *72*, 73
Cutlers Gardens 43, 52, 70

Derbyshire, Nick 32
Dowson, Philip 43, 47, 48
Duffy, Frank 70, 100
Dunn, Michael 96

Eastern Counties Railway 18
Edis, Colonel R.W. 24
English Heritage 93, 100
Eurostar 31
Euston Arch 28, *28*
Euston, destruction of 28–31
Everyman Cinema 116, *116*, *117*

Foggo, Peter 34, 40, *40*, 43, 46, 48, 52, 56, 59, 63, 66, 70, 73, 77, 79, 91, 100, 121

Gay, John 20
Gee, Emily 95, 96, 11–12
GIC 40
Gilbert Scott, George 22, 31
GLC 31
Graham, Bruce 56
Great Eastern Hotel 22–24, *23*, 31
Great Eastern Railway 18, 22
Greycoat, Rosehaugh 59, 60, 63, 66, 67, 70, 73, 77, 84
Gun Wharf, Chatham (Arup) *41*, 47

Hackney Council 60 – SERACH FIND
Hamilton, Lord Claud 22

Hannay, Patrick 77
Historic England 11, 93, 94, 95, 96, 100
Hobbs, Bob 43
Horizon Factory 44–45, 46, *46–47*
Hospital of St Mary of Bethlehem 15
Hunt, Jeremy 93

Jenkins, Simon 32
Josef Gartner GmbH 59, 73

Kennet, Lord 31

Lipton, Sir Stuart 34, 40, 46, 47, 48, 52, 56, 59, 63, 67, 73
listing of 1 Finsbury Avenue 93–96, 100
Liverpool Street Station 15, 22, 28, *30*, 31, *32*, *32*, *33*, *34*, *35*
Lloyd's of London 47, *72*
LNWR 18, 20
Lockyer, David 95
London and Blackwall railway 18
London Workhouse 15

Malcolmson, Bill 52
Meadows, Michael 79, 96
Metropolitan line 18
Midland Grand Hotel 22, 28, 31
Miller, Maria 93
Milligan, Spike 31
Monaghan, Paul 100

Nairn, Ian 25
North London Railway 18, 20

Ove Arup & Partners 43

Paxton, Joseph *72*, 73

Piano, Renzo 63, 76–77
Pindar Mansion *24*, 25
Pindar, Sir Paul 15, 25
Pompidou Centre 77

railways, development of 18–25
Reform Club 52, *56*
Ritblat, John 59, 60
Robinson & Partners 31
Robinson, Fitzroy 32, 34
Robinson, Patrick 60, 63
Roche, Kevin 56
Rogers, Richard *72*, 73, 77
Rowe & Pitman 77, 84
Rush Hour sculpture *120*

St Pancras Station 31
Sears Tower, Chicago 56
Second World War 28
Seifert, Richard 43, 52
Siedentopf, Hans 73
Skead, Peter 52

Skidmore, Owings and Merrill (SOM) 56
Strickland, Chris 79
Studio Myerscough *113*, *114–115*, *118–119*, 123
Sugden, Derek 43

Taylor, Ian 52, 57, 59
Taylor, Tony 52, 70, 77
Twentieth Century Society 91, 93

Vickers, Bruce 52

Webb, Nigel 79, 94, 95, 96, 121
Whitecross Place *111*
Wiggins Teape 46, 47, 48
 Gateway buildings 46, 47, *48*, *49*, 56, 59, 76
Wilson, Edmund 22
Wilson, Geoffrey 40
Wimpey and Taylor Woodrow 31
Winter, Les 52
Wiseman, Michael 79

Zunz, Jack 47

ACKNOWLEDGEMENTS & IMAGE CREDITS

I am grateful to British Land for commissioning this book, marking the completion of a key element in the renaissance and renewal of Broadgate as a dynamic business quarter for the 21st century – thanks are due to Chris Grigg, Nigel Webb, Michael Meadows and Adrian Penfold for their support and for invaluable briefings on the project.

Sir John Ritblat, Honorary President and formerly Chairman and Chief Executive of British Land, provided invaluable insights into the genesis of the project.

Sir Stuart Lipton, client for the original project, gave generously of his time to discuss the evolution of what was, at the time, a remarkably bold venture that was a milestone in the development of commercial architecture in Britain.

At Arup, Michael Beavan, David Pearce, Jo Ronaldson and Suzanne Harb offered insights into the history of the project and the recent renewal of the building and provided access to the practice's archives.

Thanks are due to a number of key players in the project for sharing with me their memories and reflections. I am grateful to Rab Bennetts, Paul Lewis, Ann Minogue, Patrick Robinson, Chris Strickland, Ian Taylor and Tony Taylor for their support and for giving generously of their time.

Emily Gee and Michael Dunn of Historic England briefed me on the complex negotiations underlying the renewal of a remarkable 20th-century listed building. Susie Barson provided access to Historic England's archives. Peter Rees and Annie Hampson briefed me on the evolution of 1 Finsbury Avenue and on its landmark renewal in the context of City of London planning policies.

At Allford Hall Monaghan Morris, the architectural practice for the refurbishment project, the team led by Paul Monaghan included Adrian Williams, Laura Stephenson and Tom Wells.

Finally, thanks go to Val Rose, Anna Norman and Rochelle Roberts at Lund Humphries for their painstaking work on producing this book.

I should like to dedicate this book to the memory of Peter Foggo (1930-1993), the architect who did so much to change the face of commercial architecture in Britain.

IMAGE CREDITS

The publisher would like to thank the copyright holders for granting permission to reproduce the images illustrated. Every attempt has been made to trace accurate ownership of copyrighted images. Any errors or omissions will be corrected in subsequent editions provided notification is sent to the publisher.

© AHMM: figures 35, 36, 37, 38, 40-43, 47, 48, 54, 64-70; photos by Gareth Gardner: Frontispiece and figures 60, 76, 82; photos by Rob Parish: figures 44, 51, 55-57; photos by Tim Soar: 52, 53, 58, 59, 61, 63, 71-75, 77, 79, 80, 81, 83-88.

© Architectural Press Archive / RIBA Collections: figure 17.

© Arup Associates: figures 18-32, 39, 69, 78.

© British Land: figure 62.

© Richard Bryant: figure 49.

© London Metropolitan Archives, City of London: figures 1 (ref: 1501), 2 (ref: 316254), 3 (ref: 316244), 4 (ref: 232368), 5 (ref: 4114), 6 (ref: 55068), 7 (ref: 319807), 8 (ref: 232647), 9 (ref: 232877), 14, 33 (ref: 232877), 50 (ref: 340623).

© courtesy Network Rail: figure 15.

First published in 2020 by Lund Humphries

Lund Humphries
Office 3, Book House
261A City Road
London EC1V 1JX
UK
www.lundhumphries.com

1 Finsbury Avenue © Kenneth Powell, 2020

All rights reserved

ISBN: 978–1–84822–372–1

A Cataloguing-in-Publication record for this book is available from the British Library.

All rights reserved. No part of this publication may be reproduced, stored in a retrieval system or transmitted in any form or by any means, electrical, mechanical or otherwise, without first seeking the permission of the copyright owners and publishers.

Every effort has been made to seek permission to reproduce the images in this book. Any omissions are entirely unintentional, and details should be addressed to the publishers.

Kenneth Powell has asserted his right under the Copyright, Designs and Patent Act, 1988, to be identified as the Author of this Work.

Front cover: Photo by Tim Soar for AHMM

Copy-edited by Alison Hill
Designed by TSOWC, London
Set in Berthold Akzidenz Grotesk
Printed in Wales

In association with